Singing in Musical Theatre demystifies individual work that is generally unseen by the public or even by other singing teachers—a generous act of the selected teachers, and also of Joan Melton, with her subtle and pointed questions that elicit full and illuminating answers.

Catherine Fitzmaurice, Founder of Fitzmaurice Voicework

There is no other book on the market that surveys the pedagogical practices of internationally recognized professional singing teachers. . . The book is structurally cohesive, soundly researched, and written by an author with a proven track record, who is a leading authority in the voice, singing, and acting fields.

Michael Lugering, author of *The Expressive Actor: Integrated Voice, Movement, and Acting Training*

Music theatre singing stands at the crossroads of both classical and contemporary voice training. Joan Melton's new book explores this central issue for singers and singing teachers alike, providing lively insight into the state of knowledge and practicing pedagogy in this field. Highly recommended for anyone interested in teaching and learning about singing.

Dr. Rowena Cowley, Lecturer in Voice and Pedagogy, Sydney Conservatorium of Music

D1169286

Singing
in Musical Theatre

THE TRAINING OF
SINGERS AND ACTORS

JOAN MELTON

ALLWORTH PRESS
NEW YORK

82607391

11   10   09   08   07   5   4   3   2   1

Published by Allworth Press
An imprint of Allworth Communications, Inc.
10 East 23rd Street, New York, NY 10010

Cover design by Derek Bacchus
Interior design by Mary Belibasakis
Page composition/typography by Integra Software Services, Pvt., Ltd., Pondicherry, India

Library of Congress Cataloging-in-Publication Data

Melton, Joan.
   Singing in musical theatre : the training of singers and actors / Joan Melton ; foreword by Angela Punch McGregor.
       p. cm.
   Includes index.
   ISBN-13: 978-1-58115-482-5 (pbk.)
   ISBN-10: 1-58115-482-8 (pbk.)
   1. Musical theater—Instruction and study.   2. Singing—Instruction and study.   3. Voice teachers—Interviews.
   I. Title.

   MT956.M45 2007
   782.1'4143—dc22

                                                           2007003757

Printed in Canada

Contributors

ELISABETH HOWARD

WENDY LeBORGNE

JOAN LADER

JEANNETTE LoVETRI

MARY SAUNDERS-BARTON

NEIL SEMER

MARY HAMMOND

PENNI HARVEY-PIPER

GILLYANNE KAYES

LISA RYAN-McLAUGHLIN

JASON BARRY-SMITH

DEBBIE PHYLAND

JEAN CALLAGHAN

PAT WILSON

AMANDA COLLIVER

LIZ PASCOE

Contents

FOREWORD

*I*n 1995, I began a traumatic three-year project of training to become an actor who could sing. They were holding auditions for the musical *Sunset Boulevard*. A colleague foolishly remarked that it was a role I could and should play! Always up for a challenge, I decided to find a singing teacher who could quiet my nerves, and who could reassure me through every neurotic comment I would make about my throat, my vocal cords, my tone-deaf ear, my posture, my range, and so on. On top of that, this teacher would have to calmly coach and guide me from simple scales to a major role in a musical within twelve months.

I saw a poster advertising singing lessons on the front window of the Da Capo music store in Glebe, Sydney. In small letters at the bottom of the ad, it said: Tutor, Rita Hunter CBE!

To jump to the end of what is really a most unusual tale—where I could be treated to an aria from *Madama Butterfly* at 10:00 in the morning, and at such close range I would literally weep for the privilege of it—I ended up forming a friendship with one of the greatest Wagnerian sopranos ever to walk this earth. This great singer and technician gave me an appreciation for the human voice I had never had in thirty years in the theatre. I will never sing Brunhilde, but I now have a far greater appreciation for the infinite possibilities of the vocal instrument.

Let me say that this book is an excellent and original voice manual. Joan's research gives the reader entirely new information about vocal technique because of the wide variety of teaching methods exampled here. I have long held the belief that the young acting voice can benefit immeasurably via the strategies and techniques of singing training. For both singer and actor, the voice remains the same muscles that must be stretched, relaxed, toned, warmed, exercised, rested, adjusted, treated vigorously, and treated with tenderness. After all, singing is acting on pitch!

—ANGELA PUNCH MCGREGOR

ACKNOWLEDGMENTS

*F*irst and most especially, I want to thank each of the sixteen contributors to this book. Their willingness to participate in the project, along with their generosity and expertise, make this a very special volume indeed. Each interviewee not only made time in an incredibly busy schedule for the interview itself, but also reviewed the written transcript and provided additional information to complete the work.

Secondly, I am deeply indebted to colleagues on three continents for their generous support and willingness to read parts of the manuscript. Thanks particularly to Jenny West and Angela Punch McGregor (Sydney); Katharine and Peter Watts (Auckland); Kevin Matherick (Carmarthen, Wales); Evelyn Carol Case, Maria Cominis, David Nevell, Kenneth Tom, Steve Magana, and Jim Volz (Cal State Fullerton); Chris Smith (San Juan Capistrano); Michael Lugering (Las Vegas); and Dan Kern (Philadelphia) for their positive comments, invaluable suggestions, and unflagging encouragement.

Special thanks to my students Noah Gillett, Lesley McKinnell, and Carly Menkin for their willingness to demonstrate the exercises in Chapter 19, and to Michael Puoci for photography.

Finally, my sincerest thanks to Nicole Potter-Talling, senior editor at Allworth Press, for her immediate and enthusiastic response to my vision, and her wisdom and guidance throughout the publication process.

—JOAN MELTON

INTRODUCTION

*A*s more and more classical singers consider the possibility of branching out into non-classical singing, and as actors acknowledge the very real possibility of getting more work if they can sing, musical theatre becomes a particularly attractive option for both groups. Yet the breadth of training and skill that is essential for musical theatre performance frequently comes as a surprise. For example, being a "triple threat" means *lots* of regular physical activity in the form of dance classes, movement work, theatre voice training, and, of course, actor training, in addition to regular lessons with a singing teacher and/or coach.

Singing for musical theatre is enormously demanding. It requires the ability to handle a wide variety of vocal genres, as well as the robust good health to do eight shows a week on a regular basis. *Singing in Musical Theatre* brings to one volume the insights and training perspectives of some of the most influential teachers of singing for musical theatre in the world today, through a series of personal interviews conducted in the United States, the United Kingdom, and Australia. Each of the master teachers interviewed has students and/or clients working in major theatres and/or touring productions in the United States, Great Britain, and/or Australia, as well as in other parts of the world. Each interviewee has been asked: (1) to discuss six major elements of voice training that relate directly to theatre voice: alignment, breathing, range, resonance, articulation, and connection, or the acting dimension; and (2) to relate her or his approach to voice science and to the movement-based work that is a core element of actor training. The interviews are presented in the order in which they were done, spring through fall of 2004.

Throughout the interviews, musical theatre performance emerges as an important connecting link between classical training for the singer and drama school training for the actor. Thus, the final chapters of the book compare the respective views set forth in the interviews, discuss perceived cultural differences in perspective and approach, and relate specific methods of teaching directly to theatre voice.

Music and theatre come together in extraordinary ways both in opera and in musical theatre. Even in nonmusical productions, actors sing—with or without training—and the most interesting recitalists are often singers who act—with or without training. Yet in the training process, singers and actors frequently live very different lives and take on perspectives that separate, rather than integrate, their work as performers. Singers, for example, spend hundreds of hours alone in a practice room and may feel a certain separateness, even when they are part of an ensemble. Individual competition among musicians can be fierce, and, in the classical field particularly, aural models of perfection are ever-present in the singer's conscious imagination. Likewise, actors spend preparatory time alone, training the instrument, doing research, learning lines, mastering dialects, and developing the physical details of characterization; at the same time, they may share these activities with other members of the theatre community. Whereas singers train one on one with a technician and/or a coach, actors usually learn their craft in a group setting, and even the simplest exercise or vocalise for the actor is about communicating.

One of the first things an actor learns is that the most important person on the stage is the other actor, or the partner. So the concept of *other consciousness* is a key element in actor training. Singers, on the other hand, tend to focus on the sound, which can easily pull their attention inward or, at best, divide that attention between the partner and the self. One of the reasons stage actors train so thoroughly in every form of vocal noisemaking (e.g., speaking, laughing, crying, shouting, screaming) is that their attention must *not* be on the sound when they are acting. Therefore, they must have a technique that is extremely solid. Indeed, a major problem for actors who are required to sing without training is that *that* part of their technique is not secure. So they may, of necessity, focus inward and become self-conscious because they don't know what they're doing. Likewise, singers who *sound* beautiful in sung parts of a drama may become self-conscious and uncomfortable on spoken lines because that aspect of their technique is not secure. Indeed, it is often little more than what they use in ordinary conversation if they have not had the opportunity to make the technical connections between speaking and singing on stage. In addition, the physicality of their acting is frequently limited by a lack of movement training.

Music and theatre might easily come together long before the advent of rehearsals and performances, and if they did, singers and actors would stand to benefit enormously. More overlap in the training process would mean greater ease and skill in performance, and this book is an attempt to facilitate one aspect of that overlap.

Musical theatre and theatre voice have been paired for several reasons: (1) The sung material that actors most frequently encounter, and with which they usually audition, is from musical theatre; (2) the palette of colors, or the variety of vocal sounds now being required of musical theatre singers, parallels a similar variety of spoken sounds with which the actor has trained for a much longer period of time historically; (3) the common ground for singers and actors includes strong similarities in technical approach to the vocal instrument, especially in musical theatre; and (4) the acting dimension is central to both singing and acting. That said, there is a rich and expanding body of material that relies primarily on sound and sensation, rather than on the communication of a linear story, ideas, or even feelings, as in some pop/rock musicals, performance art, physical theatre, and experimental pieces that continually stretch the boundaries of sound and movement for the sheer joy of doing so.

GUIDELINES FOR USING THIS BOOK

For many readers, simply browsing through the interviews will yield fascinating insights. Checking out differences in approach to specific aspects of voice training—for example, breathing, alignment, articulation, and resonance—will also be enlightening and useful. Cross-cultural differences observed through the interviews can provide practical information for theatre professionals who work in more than one part of the world. And, finally, the privilege of interacting vicariously with each of these dynamic teachers will be a valuable experience in itself.

Beyond the interviews and directly related to the interconnectedness of musical theatre and theatre voice are the final chapters of the book, which synthesize the material in specific and practical ways. For some readers, this is the logical place to start, so that the interviews then become an invaluable follow-up, as well as a remarkable tool for personal exploration and research.

Individual conclusions are both inevitable and desirable. Therefore, regardless of your approach, you will draw your own analogies and make your own pedagogical and performance connections. My hope in putting it all together is that this book will set off a spark, inspire a leap in communication, and open doors to performance possibilities, as it celebrates the multifaceted capabilities of the vocal instrument in the context of theatre performance.

PART I

Interviews,
UNITED STATES

1. ELISABETH HOWARD

It was Saturday afternoon and I listened to the Met broadcast as I drove along that fantastic, winding road through mountainous countryside west of Los Angeles. The deal was that we'd do the interview as soon as the opera was over and before Liz had to leave for a late-afternoon engagement.

I parked at the top of the hill and walked down. The house was as spectacular as the view—spacious, elegant. And a magnificent ebony grand caught my eye as we moved quickly from the teaching studio into the sitting room adjoining the kitchen. There I placed my recording equipment on the coffee table, and for the next hour or so Elisabeth Howard spoke with incredible energy and enthusiasm about her career, her students, her method of teaching, and her ongoing presentations in the US and abroad.

Royal Photo Studio

Liz Howard has been called a "vocal chameleon." Her expertise and ability to sing in styles from blues, R & B, and country western, to jazz, musical theatre, and opera is unparalleled. She is both a glorious coloratura soprano and a belter! In addition, Liz is a songwriter, actress, international clinician, and a master teacher of voice. She is the author of Sing! *(2005), and the founder/director of the Vocal Power Academy in Los Angeles, California.*

PERSPECTIVE

*Will you say something about your background and about what
influenced or informed your approach to teaching?*

I began studying piano at age five, cello at age ten, and voice at age
fifteen. I come from an Italian background where a love of the arts
permeated my existence. Every Saturday, my family listened to the
Met broadcasts and I would sing along, loving and imitating what
I heard.

My immediate family influenced and encouraged me to teach piano,
and then voice. My mother taught ballet, tap, and ballroom. My father
taught violin and piano. And two uncles taught guitar and piano at the
studio for my mother's school, the Lanza School of Dance and Music.
One day my mother scheduled a voice lesson for me to teach on a
Saturday morning and informed me that I was going to teach a seven-
year-old. I protested, saying I didn't know how to teach, but went along
with the idea just to appease my mother at least for one lesson—or so
I thought. Instead, I found that I loved teaching voice from the very
first minute that I worked with this eager seven-year-old, blond, curly-
haired girl that my mother scheduled for me. And I've been teaching
ever since!

My aunt taught me to play Bach on the piano when I was seven. I also
had a great attraction to the rock and roll music that was just beginning
to surface at that time, and, at the piano, I sang and wrote pop songs.
In high school I studied classical voice with Julia Heinz, the wife of
Hans Heinz, who was teaching at Juilliard at that time. Mr. Heinz heard
me sing and said, "Keep it up and you'll come to Juilliard," and that's
what I did. I supported myself through Juilliard by teaching voice for
my mother's school, privately in Manhattan, and at Hunter College in
New York City.

*Do you work with students on classical as well as musical theatre
repertoire? Do you teach vocal styles other than classical and/or
musical theatre?*

Yes, I work extensively on classical and musical theatre. Besides classical
and musical theatre, I teach jazz, rock, R&B, blues, and alternative.

What exactly do you mean by alternative?

Alternative is a term used to describe in music what *abstract* means in art. It isn't middle of the road pop, R&B, or jazz, though it may have elements of R&B and jazz. Artists like Sarah McLachlan, Alanis Morissette, and Tori Amos are alternative artists. Their songs have less structure than ABA, are free flowing, and seem through composed, stream-of-consciousness, I would say. The subjects are usually very introspective, sometimes poetic, dark, and personal.

How would you describe the vocal requirements for singers in musical theatre today? How have those requirements changed over the years and where do you think they're going?

The demands on the musical theatre performer are greater than ever. For auditions, a singer may be required to sing an operatic aria one day and a rock song the next. But I believe we are heading back to some form of specialization in musical theatre, since there are so many styles being presented in new shows and revivals. For example, for women, there's the light belt/soprano in shows like *Thoroughly Modern Millie* and *Songs for a New World*, and the stronger, heftier weighted vocal requirements of shows like *Wild Party* and *Mamma Mia*. Then we have an almost operatic approach to "You Don't Know This Man," from *Parade* and "Think of Me," from *Phantom*. I think it's a little easier for a man to cross over *vocally*, from a song like "Younger than Springtime," from *South Pacific*, for example, to "One Song Glory," from *Rent*.

Crossing over in style is a different matter. In classical singing, we interpret Handel very differently from Puccini, and it's no different in musical theatre. The R&B style in *Dreamgirls* and *The Life* is very different from the pop sounds of *Rent*. And if any of these shows had bona fide "pop" songs in them, they'd be on the charts, on the radio, and in a video on MTV. The so-called "pop" shows are really pop-*influenced*, I would say. Except for songs like "I Don't Know How to Love Him," from *Jesus Christ Superstar*, and "Memory" from *Cats*, very few pop-style songs from shows have actually been accepted as pop by the public. "Hopelessly Devoted to You," from *Grease*, was a hit on the charts for Olivia Newton-John, but was written after the stage show for the movie with the intention of becoming a pop hit, which it did.

I feel the trend in musical theatre is going to go back to specialization. Students have to explore all the styles they enjoy singing, and then decide which styles and sounds they do the best and learn all the repertoire for that voice type. For example, the Julie Andrews voice type is not also the Ethel Merman voice type. If a singer goes into an audition with an Ethel Merman-type song and sings with a Julie Andrews-type voice, she's wasting her time. There will be an Ethel Merman-type singer who will sing an Ethel Merman-type song and get a call back, if that's what the casting people are looking for. It's really like opera in that sense. You've got to know your Fach (voice type) and sing and perfect that repertoire. A good outside ear will help—your teacher or vocal coach for starters.

Why do you teach what you teach? What drives you? What is your passion in this work?

I teach what I teach for the love of the human voice and what it can do. To experience my students' successes and to see them accomplish their dreams is what drives me. I believe that anyone can learn how to sing and sing very beautifully at *any* age and I have the need to prove this every day of my life. Every day of teaching brings new experiences and new growth for me as a teacher, singer, and person. What more could I ask from a profession?

What role does voice science, or vocal anatomy and physiology, play in your work with students or clients?

I think it's very important and exciting for us to know how things work, to know and acknowledge that some people aren't born with a naturally good voice, and to know that with clear and logical explanations we can take the *mystery* out of singing. We can control the sounds that we desire with our minds, muscle coordination, and ear, and we can do it consistently, every single time, and not only with a "hope and a prayer."

Do you use any recording equipment in your studio? Do you teach microphone techniques?

I have a tape recorder to record lessons, and a "Singing Machine" that plays CDs and tapes with the capability of transposing up or down seven half-steps. I use two microphones for non-classical songs, one at the piano for me and one for the student. Microphone techniques are easy and can be taught in five minutes, but the student must practice.

THE TRAINING

*Where do you start? What are the vital signs you check right away
when a student comes to you? What are the foundational aspects of
training to which you regularly attend?*

I start with breathing and support, moving on to creating clear, nonbreathy
tones, then the four colors (resonances) that I teach, then power and projec-
tion, head voice, chest voice, blending registers, the mix, vibrato, and so on.
I check for a good ear, the ability to concentrate, energy, and the desire to
sing beautifully.

Will you talk about the four colors, or resonances, that you mentioned?

I work with head, nasal, mouth, and chest resonances, which I refer to as
colors. We word-paint with our colors, letting the emotions dictate. For
example, if I were singing "Stormy Weather," I would most likely choose
a warm and deep color to best describe that image. Or if I were singing
about a sunny day, I would use more mask/nasal for a brighter sound.
We practice these four colors separately, first in exercises and then apply
them to our songs.

*What do you expect to observe in a singer who is well trained or in
a performer who sings well, with or without training?*

I appreciate vocal freedom, expression, and a love of singing and the
music.

*Granted, the journey is different from one singer to another, but would
you say something about how students might get from A to B, or from
their first lessons with you to a solid professional technique?*

They must first learn many vocal techniques, systematically, from breathing, support, vocal colors, registers, mixed voice, vibrato, coloratura for
classical and non-classical, blues and pentatonic scales for non-classical.
These techniques and various exercises are designed to give a singer the
freedom to sing in any style he or she wishes. The next step is to develop
a personal style for non-classical, and for classical singers, to polish the
various songs and arias. Then it all comes together when they learn how to
present themselves at an audition or performance.

*In the answers to earlier questions, you have touched on some, if not
all, of the six aspects of training listed below:*

*Alignment, Breathing, Range, Resonance, Articulation,
Connection (the Acting Dimension)*

*Now, from the perspective of your own approach, would you comment
specifically on each of these elements, to whatever extent and in
whatever order you choose?*

I work with body *alignment* with regard to breathing, support, power, pro-
jection, dynamics, and presentation. Breathing and support coordination is
the first technique I teach. With good breathing and support habits, a
singer can build the rest of the techniques that go into the freedom to
express the lyrics and music.

Range is expanded and stretched gradually from the highest to the
lowest note in every voice. I expect all my students to develop at least
a three-octave range, no matter what their age or singing style.

Resonance is paramount in my teaching. My philosophy, to quote the
great cellist Pablo Casals, is, "Every note deserves to live." Color, quality,
expression, vibrato, and dynamics, with a good foundation in breath control, are basic to my teaching.

Articulation. Pronunciation and articulation are very important in the
determination of style. For example, articulation for a Mozart aria on a
stage, is worlds apart from singing blues on a mike.

Connection. Solid technique must be so automatic and free that the
singer can interpret a song or aria every single time, as if it were the first
time he or she were singing those words. Every single word must be
explored and personal. The singer must do the homework. Each song is
a monologue and must be treated as such, the way we do in acting.
We must use our five senses to give a full and sensuous performance.
Singers need training in performance. In the Vocal Power Academy, we
give performance workshops, which include microphone technique, acting, movement, and image, to prepare singers for the stage. Musical
theatre actors and actresses need to know how to audition, and we work
on audition material in the workshops. Then the singers are presented in
showcases.

You mentioned the word image. *What do you mean by* image *in this context?*

We discuss and explore the vocal style of each singer and what would be appropriate on stage in terms of hairstyle, dress, pants, suit, makeup, and the like. What does the singer want the audience to know about them—casual, funky, sophisticated? We also make sure that if the song is going to be performed in a dress and high heels, that the singer practices in a dress and high heels. Or if the singer is doing a country song, it might be appropriate to wear jeans and boots for practice. In other words, no surprises the day of performance.

Again, from your perspective, how do these individual aspects of training relate to one another (1) in the learning process, and (2) in performance?

Technical skills come first. The voice is an instrument and we learn how to play it. The mind and the muscle coordination must work together, and the ear must guide the sounds. All these elements come together to create beautiful sounds that are full of passion and personal expression. I tell my students to always sing with passion, not only in songs and arias, but in scales and arpeggios; I tell them that even one single note must live.

Do you have additional comments you would like to make?

I believe that anyone at any age can learn to sing. The Vocal Power Method is a step-by-step, systematic approach using techniques that I've developed over many years of singing and teaching, which enable a singer to be a "vocal acrobat." Techniques that set my approach apart from other methods are: "vibrato on the breath"; the "shimmer vibrato"; the two different "mixed voices"—head mix and chest mix, for the higher range and for safe belting; work on dynamics; and using the "four vocal colors" for variation in expression. For developing blues, R&B, rock, and jazz styles, we don't only use major scales, but we use the blues and pentatonic scales as exercises for *licks*, and improvisation for creating the *legit* sound in pop, jazz, rock, and R&B. There is no mystery, only *joy*!

PUBLICATIONS

Howard, E. 2005. *Born to Sing*, with video or DVD. Los Angeles: Vocal Power.

———. 2005. *The ABCs of Vocal Harmony*. Los Angeles: Vocal Power.

———. 2005. *Sing!* Los Angeles: Vocal Power.

Web site: www.vocalpowerinc.com

2. WENDY LEBORGNE

Photography by J. C. Penny Studio

Dr. Wendy LeBorgne brought an unusual perspective to the New York conference of the Voice and Speech Trainers Association (VASTA) in the summer of 2003. As a singer and musical theatre specialist, she had done outstanding research in the area of belting, and as a practicing speech-language pathologist, she worked daily with professional actors and singers. In addition, she was one of the most dynamic and well-organized speakers we had ever encountered! I'd met Wendy earlier in the summer at a conference in Philadelphia and had since read her dissertation on belting. Now it was spring break and I was headed for Cincinnati. Wendy met me at the airport, and for the next day and a half I observed her work with patients and clients.

Dr. LeBorgne is an honorary Assistant Professor at the University of Cincinnati in the College of Allied Health Sciences and serves as a voice consultant to the Cincinnati Conservatory of Music. She is an associate editor for the VASTA Journal in the area of singing, and serves as vice president of the Ohio Voice Association.

PERSPECTIVE

*Will you say something about your background and about what
influenced or informed your approach to teaching?*

My background is in musical theatre. I have a BFA in musical theatre
from Shenandoah Conservatory in Winchester, Virginia. At the end of my
senior year at Shenandoah, I took a class in vocal pedagogy, taught by
Dr. Jeannette Og. One of our assignments was to choose from a list of
pedagogy texts or voice science texts and read them, and, for whatever
reason, I picked Bob Sataloff's book on *Care of the Professional Voice*. I think
I actually read it cover to cover and became really interested in the aspects
of high-risk vocal performers' minimizing injury and maximizing performance. I think of them as professional athletes. So I went back to
school and got my master's degree in speech-language pathology from the
University of Cincinnati, because they also have a strong music
department and I hoped I would be able to continue some singing training as well. For my doctorate, I was lucky enough to be able to self-design
my program, which was based on an article that appeared in the *Journal
of Voice*. The article outlined a prospective degree in "arts medicine." So
my official major, communication sciences and disorders, consisted of
studies in voice lab instrumentation, treatment of head and neck cancer,
voice science, and professional voice use. The cognate for my doctorate is
actually in vocal pedagogy, and the majority of that coursework was completed through the conservatory. It included Alexander Technique and
vocal lit class, diction classes, private lessons, and then a self-directed doc-
toral lecture-recital. My minor was neuroscience. That coursework was
done at UC medical school, and included gross anatomy with the medical
school students, and neuroanatomy. I took additional coursework in exercise physiology and psychopharmacology. The university and individual
professors were gracious enough to allow me to take some of the best from
many departments within the university in order to create this unique
degree.

My interest really lies in looking at, evaluating, and researching high-
level performers. Getting to the heart of what they do. What makes them
hire-able, and then how do we train those traits in the most healthy way
possible, so they're getting the most bang for their buck while minimizing
any detrimental effects?

Do you work with students on classical as well as musical theatre repertoire? Do you teach vocal styles other than classical and/or musical theatre?

I do have both. I guess I should qualify by saying I had a private studio for four or five years when I was working on my doctorate. When I finished my degree and started seeing patients full time in private practice, I phased out my private studio and now only do individual coaching and some technical work. Those students are primarily involved in musical theatre, as that's where I feel my strengths lie. I work with a lot of classical singers as well, but mostly from a rehab perspective. The majority of the classical singers already have teachers and coaches, as do many of the musical theatre singers, and my role is to help them get vocally healthy. I also work with country singers, contemporary Christian singers, and some pop/rock singers.

Mostly in rehab, or as their teacher?

Mostly in rehab, but many non-classical singers don't have teachers. So if they need a teacher, and many of them do, I will help them get vocally healthy, provide a technical evaluation of their singing, provide them with some suggestions/exercises/vocalises to get them started in the right direction, and then help them find a voice teacher.

How would you describe the vocal requirements for singers in musical theatre today? How have those requirements changed over the years and where do you think they're going?

For music theatre today, I feel that singers need to have a unique voice. It doesn't necessarily have to be the prettiest voice, or the most technically advanced; I don't think those things are absolutely necessary. Rather, I think it is a unique, "freak of nature" voice that makes it interesting to listen to. Today's musical theatre composers are starting to push the vocal boundaries of what the human voice is capable of. Inevitably, there is a singer out there who can do what composers are writing and then they write bigger and better songs. I think that we are getting into an age of vocal acrobatics. I envision composers and directors saying, "Let's see what people can do vocally. Let me write this and see what they (the singers) can do." And then when the singers get into performance situations, they take their own artistic liberties with the composer's blessing and they just do some amazing things with their instrument.

Today's music theatre singers must have an excellent command of their instrument. They need to know how it works, what it can do, how to improve the flexibility and agility so they can do those vocal acrobatics easily, or at least seemingly easily. Don't misunderstand: I don't necessarily believe that what they are doing is easy, but I think today's singers are like dancers; they make it look unbelievably easy so that we all think we can do it.

Why do you teach what you teach? What drives you? What is your passion in this work?

I love seeing and hearing people do things that are vocally amazing, and I want to figure out how to make that happen for other people in a healthy manner. I think that there is a tremendous amount of discipline in the performing arts and seeing these singers create art is my reward. They have great personalities and I love working with them. And, for me, dealing with injured voices, it's personally satisfying to be able to help singers who feel as if their career may be in jeopardy recover to the point where they are performing eight shows a week. It can be emotionally draining for a performer when this is all they have ever wanted to do and now they can't do it because they are injured. To be able to help facilitate healing, get them back to their pre-injury status, and see them perform is amazing! So I love that part of it. This is what drives me.

What role does voice science, or vocal anatomy and physiology, play in your work with students or clients?

Although I have a good understanding of how the laryngeal mechanism works, when I study or take a lesson, I think imagery is a tool that helps to incorporate the science with the art. I know that if I need to brighten my sound, I need to relax my tongue and bring it forward, but I don't typically think of those details when performing. Rather, an image of an inverted megaphone or "placing" the sound "in the mask" is often more beneficial for me. You can get too hung up in the science, but don't get me wrong, I still think it's important.

For my clients and students I teach voice as I would any instrument. For example, if you take a clarinet out of the case, the first thing you need to learn is how to put it together. So we talk about appropriate body alignment. Specifically, how do you put your instrument (your posture) together and what's the power generator (the respiratory system)? What do you think would happen if you compromised your power generator, if you didn't have enough power? We discuss, to some degree, the respiratory, laryngeal, and articulatory anatomy and physiology, and if there is an injury involved, we may discuss it a bit further. I'm lucky in the fact that we have a strobe unit in my office, so the singers are able to see the anatomy I am talking about, which makes a huge difference. A picture is often worth a thousand words. I also use lots of diagrams and models. One thing that I find really important is the use of good anatomical models and accurate references.

Voice science has provided us the tools to be able to analyze voices to some degree. However, one thing I have learned in doing research is that it is extremely difficult to quantify art. You always have this X factor in the artist that is not easily quantifiable. Although I can look at the acoustics of an instrument or the anatomy of an instrument, you can't quantify that higher ability, or that intrinsic, amazing nature of the artist.

In communicating with singers about how the voice works, do you find you're sometimes dispelling myths?

Absolutely. I always ask my students, "How do you think your voice works?" This provides me with a starting point, because some people have a very good grasp and we don't need to go back to basics. With others, we need to start at the beginning with respect to respiration, phonation, and resonance. I find one of the biggest problems is that there is a lot of semantic confusion. The terminology among voice professionals—whether it's voice pathologists, singing teachers, or vocal coaches—is not the same. Unfortunately, this often results in the student getting confused, when, in actuality, everyone may be talking about the exact same thing using five different terms.

Does movement or movement-based training play a role in your teaching?

It does. I like Alexander Technique quite a lot, perhaps because it is the type of training that I have had the most direct experience with. I feel that, especially in musical theatre, when you're having to move all the time, that you need to have a good sense of what your body does when it moves. Pilates I am a little more wary of in young singers because of the breathing techniques. I think it's a good way to confuse a young singer as far as breathing goes. Pilates is almost counterproductive initially because it is a different type of breathing. My more advanced students or clients, when they have established a good sense of breathing, can easily take a Pilates class and switch their breathing. I think Pilates is great for core strengthening.

Do you use any recording equipment in your studio? Do you teach microphone techniques?

I do. I always record them the first time I see them. For my research, and with the freshmen that I screen, all of them sing sixteen bars of an uptempo and sixteen bars of a ballad, and then they sing "The Star-Spangled Banner" in a specific key, depending on their voice type. So I have a baseline for them, and that gives me an idea of where they're coming from. I always have my students record their lessons. I think you get so much out of it if you go back and listen to it. That is the key—to go back and listen to the tape.

I also use spectography to look at voices, more as a demonstration or for research purposes than as something I use all the time. It is a great tool to see where the formants are in an /ah/ vowel, or where they are for an /i/. Certainly that's time consuming, but if there's a specific problem, I'm lucky to have the tools available. Also, it's very visible to the singer as they are manipulating things. When something is right, they are able to see it visually and feel it internally. Then they start to learn by feeling.

As for the microphone techniques, I try to teach singers to be their own advocates. Ideally, on the musical theatre stage, the best microphone would be an over the ear that comes around in front of the mouth. If that is not tolerated for whatever production, the next best mike placement is at the top of the forehead, with the third choice being an over-the-ear placement, called an ear rig, that does not come around in front of the mouth. I really don't recommend lapel microphones. Sometimes I think we still get them in high school settings, but even a lot of high schools have gone to the head-mounted microphones. If they are using hand-held microphones, like in pop singing, we want to make sure the microphones are adequate. I try to ask whether they're using a microphone that's in a stand. Are they playing guitar at the same time? Do they have the boy band microphone stance where the microphone is pointed up towards the sky? Are they doing anything unusual with their neck when they are singing into a microphone? So, depending on their current microphone use, I may do some modification.

I tell all my singers to make sure the sound engineer is their best friend, because if they are having a bad day, the microphone levels may need to be adjusted. They need to make sure that the mikes are properly placed and cleaned and that the screens are cleaned. I do a lot of counseling on microphone use.

THE TRAINING

Where do you start? What are the vital signs you check right away when a student comes to you? What are the foundational aspects of training to which you regularly attend?

The first thing I do when I meet a new singer is an interview. From the moment they walk in the room, my ears are automatically perked up to what they sound like, how they're standing or sitting, their personality from the standpoint of their effect, how personally invested they are. Are they willing to make changes? Are they open to new ideas, or are they very set in what they do? And what are their goals? From the interview I generally get a good sense of their speaking voice. That often tells me a lot about the daily use of the mechanism. Then I will have them sing for me. I will do my version of a voice evaluation, just to see where they are. I look at posture first, because again, it goes back to having your instrument put together correctly. When I assess that, I look at what they do when they inhale/exhale during "quiet breathing." Is that different from what they do when they phonate? Is their breathing different in the chest, middle, and head voice? Do they alter their alignment as they get higher? There's a whole list of things that I go through, a mental checklist, and I'll have them do this typically on vocalise. I typically will have them bring something in, two contrasting sixteen-bars. I am trying to assess all of these things while they are speaking and singing. The second thing I look at is breathing, independent of support, because I'm an analytical person and I like to break it down. I look at their breathing, whether it is clavicular, thoracic, or abdominal. Does it change as they go through their range? Does it change when they sing songs, versus when they are just doing vocalises? Then I look at breath support. Is it deficient? Is it late? Or is it over supported? Is it appropriate for what they're doing? Then I look at their phonation. Are they using hard glottal attacks? Are they using aspirate attacks? What are they doing at the laryngeal level (elevation/depression of the larynx)? And then, finally, looking at the resonance (the filter system), do they have jaw tension? Do they have tongue tension? Is it vowel-specific? I have a whole list of things that I assess. I look at their range. Is it restricted? I look at the inherent beauty in the instrument—at least I rate that from my personal aesthetic. Do they have what it takes, in my opinion, to reach the goals that they have set for themselves? And if they are completely unrealistic, then we have to have a conversation about realistic goals. Although with training I can help to improve their system, I may not be able to provide them with enough tools to support a career. I don't think that you can necessarily know that in one lesson, but you can get a sense of it after working with somebody for forty-five minutes or so. Those are the fundamental aspects of a first session.

What do you expect to observe in a singer who is well trained or in a performer who sings well, with or without training?

I expect to observe, probably, some uniqueness in a really well-trained singer. Tools that they will have taken from all the lessons and training, and incorporated the best parts from everyone they have studied with. They will have developed their own sense of what works for them. They may not have perfect technique by the textbooks, but I listen for health of the system, and are they getting the most out of their instrument (have they mastered it)? Because we're all different instruments and we're unique and we have different spaces that we work in inside our bodies, I don't think there's a cookbook solution to training voices. If they have found something that works for them, who am I to come in and start all over again? I think so often we start with the breathing. I don't care how long you've studied, that's where everybody wants to start. Is that a bad thing? No, but I find in my really experienced professional voice users, they know what they're supposed to do, they know what works for them, and if they're doing eight shows a week without problems, then they're probably doing something right.

In observing my younger singers and my more beginning singers, I expect that they are going to be imitators a lot of times, and I always ask them who they listen to or who they think are good singers. That often gives me insight into what I'm going to see. If we are talking about some of the pop stars nowadays, I'm going to see something very different from somebody who listens to NPR Opera Weekend, perhaps.

Granted, the journey is different from one singer to another, but would you say something about how students might get from A to B, or from their first lessons with you to a solid professional technique?

I usually either get the class of singer who is already professional or the amateur singer who has been singing the same way forever. First of all, asking about their goals is important. Then I ask myself, "How am I going to help them achieve their goals?" because that is the bottom line and the reason they are coming to see you in the first place. After a voice analysis, I try to explain things systematically (alignment, respiration, phonation, resonance, artistry) from the standpoint of "This is where you are." Then I try to show them through examples: "When you do this, it causes your alignment to be off," and we just go through each component of voice very systematically.

I don't often use the word *change*, because I think people get defensive with *change*, but rather say something along the lines of, "These *tools* may provide you with an easier sense of voice production." Whether it be the speaking voice that we start with, or posture, or whatever it might be, certain exercises will work better for certain people. For example, if I have a coloratura soprano who has a lack of flexibility in her voice, I may start with flexibility and agility exercises, literally runs and runs and runs, and we start with a metronome. A muscle training/retraining task. If someone wants to develop a stronger middle voice or a stronger mix (because I find that, especially in female voices, that's often a problem area), I may use a messa di voce–type exercise. The messa di voce has been used for years and years to help build dynamic control in voices. Now I may add a little twist on the exercises by having them do it with an excessive frontal focus [see Figure 2-1], as opposed to mi < >. Either can work, but I feel that if we are using music theatre as our basis, I want them to get into text as soon as they can. I like to try to start with things where students are going to see improvement quickly. I want them to be successful. I think if your

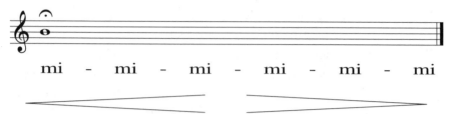

Figure 2-1

students find success in what they're doing, then they are going to return in order to get continued improvement. Success also serves as natural positive feedback, as opposed to negative reinforcement. I think when students hear, "Let's take a look at what you are doing right and maximize that," it's much more beneficial than constantly hearing, "You're doing this wrong, you're doing this wrong."

In the answers to earlier questions, you have touched on some, if not all, of the six aspects of training listed below:

Alignment, Breathing, Range, Resonance, Articulation, Connection (the Acting Dimension)

Now, from the perspective of your own approach, will you comment specifically on each of these technical elements, to whatever extent and in whatever order you choose?

Artistry, or the connection, the acting dimension is, I think, the most challenging to train, because very often I feel it's like a gifted athlete. I may be able to train a soccer player to be a better technician, but that doesn't necessarily mean that they're going to play in a professional arena. I think, on a professional level, artistry is probably the most important aspect of performance. You find your own uniqueness and make it hireable, as opposed to copying somebody else, because nobody wants to hear a copy; they want to hear the next best voice/actor.

One issue that arises with respect to *alignment* is that in music theatre you need to look good, which often requires weight lifting and training. I find, with men especially, when they're starting to strengthen their upper chest, they get this rolling forward of the shoulders due to over development of the pectoralis muscle, without counter training the trapezius. We often have a discussion about what muscles they are strengthening when they are lifting, and that it may be affecting their optimal alignment. I will try to help them find a personal trainer to give them exercises where they're still going to be building the chest, but are not getting the rolling forward of the shoulders, so that we're balancing the front and back muscles.

Core strength is essential when one has to move while singing. I don't think there is a lot of information out there right now, from a scientific standpoint, on core strength in performers. However, when performers are asked to run and jump and dance and do stage combat in costumes that may be restrictive, or they are dangling from a ceiling singing their heart out, if you don't have good core strength, I don't care how vocally strong you are, I don't care how good your breathing technique is, you're not going to survive, because you can't stabilize your body. So that's something of interest for further research, and there are specific exercises designed to train core strength and stability.

When I train *breathing*, I look at where we're starting. In a dancer, I'm going to train breathing a little differently than in an actor or a singer. I know that if dancers have been dancing for twenty years, I am not going to get them to release their abs like I will in singers—not that I don't strive for that, but I am okay with them breathing just a little bit higher. It doesn't have to be very, very low. Some dancers get it, some dancers can do it, but I think that's a rarity, rather than common.

When I'm training *range*, I think that range extension exercises are important. I think it is important to stretch to the physiological limits, not where you're going to sing in public, but physiologically your limits. Please do not assume that you sing primarily at the extremes of your range in order to increase range, but you need to touch those extreme notes if you're going to end up slightly below there for public performance. So we do range extension exercises. I use arpeggios. I will often use staccato. Especially in the upper range, I will use a very, very forward, pointed sound on /u/, so they are singing almost on a whistle, but not quite, so they take all the pressure off the larynx in order to access the upper register. Also for range, sometimes I use a running passage, as opposed to trying to separate and touch; it's going to depend on the age and ability of the singer. On low range, I'll do, typically, slides [Figure 2-2], and then how far can they go and functionally phonate? I use Vocal Function Exercises (Stemple,

Figure 2-2

Glaze, & Gerdeman, 2000) all the time, which are designed to improve the flexibility and range of the system.

In addition, I will very often do something called a voice range profile on singers, which measures intensity by frequency. There is a plethora of literature explaining how and why to do voice range profiles (Phonetograms/Stimmfeld), which are a plot of intensity and frequency of a person's voice. Anybody can do this in the voice studio. All you need is a piano and a sound-level meter, which you can purchase at Radio Shack. You have singers sing as softly, and then as loudly as they can (I use ten specific pitches throughout their range) and it gives you a graph of their voice. If they are lacking range, or if they are lacking dynamic flexibility in part of their voice, you are visually going to be able to see that. And if you do it again after six months, you can show improvement. That is a good concrete example for the singer. So, in training range, it's a tool that you can use to actually say, "Yes, you are making improvement."

If somebody has an abnormally limited range, there may be a physiological problem. That is often a red flag for me. For singers, I like to start from the top down (5-4-3-2-1 pattern), as opposed to the bottom up (1-2-3-4-5 pattern), because I feel that when you start at the top the voice doesn't carry as much weight.

Resonance-wise, I ask students to play with their resonance all the time. They need to understand how their voice works to go [demonstrates nasal to open sound] without altering anything but their resonance. It's amazing the number of singers who find it difficult to produce a nasal sound without excessive tension. Most singers can get this way far back sound, but very few can get the really nasal sound. Although you would most likely never use either resonance extreme in performance (unless it is a character role), I think it is important to know what various types of resonance feel like and to understand that these are sympathetic vibrations. When you feel chest resonance, you're feeling sympathetic vibrations. When you feel resonance in your face, you're not singing into your face; you're getting a sympathetic vibration. Some people say, "Oh I feel vibration; I'm singing through the top of my head," and that's great imagery, but it's one of my pet peeves, as a myth to dispel, that you are actually not singing through the top of your head, but rather, you are getting a sympathetic vibration.

I think that in music theatre, you must be a good actor. A skilled actor has as good a shot at a role as a singer with impeccable technique but average acting skills. So I think that's very important. And now the bottom line is you have to be a triple threat. You have to be able to dance, act, and sing, and you've got to be unique. You have to have something about you that stands out, in a positive way.

Again, from your perspective, how do these individual aspects of training relate to one another (1) in the learning process and (2) in performance?

I've compartmentalized all of these aspects and I think they must be integrated, and that's the challenge. Although students can learn to breathe properly, eliminate hard glottal attacks, maximize their resonating chambers, and learn to act, these aspects (and many others) must be incorporated into the whole package. So often in our training we compartmentalize. We go to acting class and we do scene study and we take everything apart and it is often left to the student to integrate that knowledge and put it all together. Then we go to our singing lesson, and we just work on breathing for thirty minutes. Then we go to our dance lesson and we're not allowed to let our abs out. I think you have to take the best of everything, integrate it, and then just do it.

Do you have additional comments you'd like to make?

My passion is in the arena of musical theatre. I think that bridging the gap between science and art is, in this genre, probably still in its infancy. We've done a really good job in classical music in getting a great start on what is considered vocally beautiful. But how do we measure vocal beauty? What do the exercises of the early vocal pedagogues do? Do they work, or should we toss them out the window? We haven't gotten that far yet with music theatre and we often apply things from classical literature to musical theatre when they may not be applicable or appropriate.

If we take sports as an example, very few professional-level athletes cross over into more than one sport. They are usually good in more than one sport, but, professionally speaking, there are very few who cross over. I think it's probably, realistically, the same way with singers. If you're a classical singer, you are going to train your muscles to sing that way.

You're going to develop your ear for that aesthetic. I think the same thing needs to happen in music theatre, and if we accept music theatre as a separate entity, then we begin to train it as such. Do we train jazz singers the same way we train music theatre performers? Or do we train them classically? What type of training will benefit them most? I don't know that I have the answers to those questions, but those are some thoughts.

The other thing we talked about a little bit yesterday was the registration issue and the classification of voices. From a registration standpoint, what is chest register, what is modal register, what is glottal fry, what is falsetto, what is head voice, what is mixed voice? It is a mess! And it's no wonder students are very confused, because the terminology we use in the speech science world and in the singing world is different. *Head voice* does not mean the same thing in singing as it does from the standpoint of speech science. It's very frustrating to try to work on that. The simplest perspective that I have is probably that in the lowest part of your range, the thyroarytenoid muscle is most active and the cricothyroid muscle is minorly active, say, 98 percent to 2 percent. As we get into the middle part of the voice, you should have, ideally, in a perfectly balanced world, 50 percent activity of both muscles or somewhere thereabout. And then as we transition into the upper range, you get 98 percent of cricothyroid and 2 percent of thyroarytenoid. There are thirteen muscles in the larynx, so I'm not saying those are the only two, but they are primary. I think that in music theatre we tend to use a slight bit more thyroarytenoid activity across the range. So you have a parallel line to ideal that is slightly more thyroarytenoid active. If we get too high with too much thyroarytenoid action, the voice is going to break. You may end up with this "hole" in your voice if the muscles are improperly balanced. Or you have a head voice that is not strong. So I think that you have to have a balanced instrument, but you balance it toward a little bit more bass, a little less treble, if you want to think of it that way. And from a voice classification standpoint, perhaps things like belt, legit, pop belt, jazz belt, country, twang, or whatever you want to call it, those may be more parallel to voice classifications like subrette, coloratura, and so on.

Most classical singers will sing within their Fach. They will learn the repertoire that is appropriate for their voice type. Yet in music theatre we expect them to be able to do it all. Not that they shouldn't, but very often I think that they're going to be cast as a *comic lead*, or a *legit ingénue*, and perhaps those are the vocal classifications and types of literature we should be training for those specific voices. I don't know. It's again just a thought.

PUBLICATIONS

Kelchner, L., Stemple, J., Gerdeman, B., LeBorgne, W., & Adam S. 1999. "Etiology, Pathophysiology, Treatment Choices, and Voice Results for Unilateral Adductor Vocal Fold Paralysis: A 3-Year Retrospective." *Journal of Voice* 13, no. 4: 592–601.

LeBorgne, W. "The Young Singer: Considerations for Vocal Training in Young Children Through Adolescence." American Speech Language Hearing Association, Division 3 *Newsletter* 12, no. 2 (July 2002): 14–16.

LeBorgne, W. & Weinrich, B. 2002. "Phonetogram Changes for Trained Singers Over a Nine-Month Period of Training." *Journal of Voice* 16, no. 1: 37–43.

REFERENCES

Sataloff, R. T. 2005. *Professional Voice: The Science and Art of Clinical Care.* San Diego: Plural.

Sabol, J. W., Lee, L., & Stemple, J. C. 1995. "The Value of Vocal Function Exercises in the Practice Regimen of Singers." *Journal of Voice* 9, no. 1: 27–36.

Stemple, J. C., Glaze, L. E., & Gerdeman, B. K. 2000. *Clinical Voice Pathology.* San Diego: Singular/Thomson Learning.

3. JOAN LADER

Photography by Beth Kelly

It was a cold, rainy day in New York. I arrived a bit early for my appointment with Joan Lader, had a cup of tea, and wandered through the Jewish Museum nearby, then rang the bell at the appointed time. Joan greeted me in the hall. Soon I realized we'd actually met before, when she'd participated in a workshop I taught at a summer conference, and I felt deeply honored.

For the past twenty-five years, Joan Lader has had one of New York's busiest private practices as a voice teacher and therapist. Her students and patients include some of the world's leading performers from Broadway, pop, opera, and rock and roll. Outside the studio, she has served as a vocal consultant to singers, actors, conductors, and producers on numerous recordings, as well as on film. She has guest-lectured at many prestigious colleges and universities in the United States, is on the Advisory Board at Ann Reinking's Broadway Theater Project in Tampa, Florida, and teaches regularly as a guest artist at The Lost Colony, *in North Carolina.*

PERSPECTIVE

Where and whom do you teach?

I teach in New York City, on 16th Street in this studio. I teach and treat professional singers from Broadway to pop with an emphasis on Broadway performers. Because I have a "high profile" clientele, many of whom have vocal injuries, I have to adhere to a policy of professional confidentiality. However, very often people use my name in interviews and if you were to do a search on the Web you'd see that the population is diverse, including performers such as Betty Buckley, Madonna, Frederica von Stade, Donna Murphy, and Harvey Fierstein.

Is New York your home?

I was born and raised in New York City and I've been teaching in this particular space for over twenty-five years.

Will you say something about what influenced or informed your approach to teaching?

I started, basically, as a performer and was doing musical theatre as well as voiceover work. Like most performers, I was nervous about the future and decided to return to graduate school to study speech pathology and audiology. There were very few people, at that time, treating singers with voice problems. As a matter of fact, very few people had instrumentation to view the larynx. I began attending symposiums, particularly the Voice Foundation, which was [then] based at Juilliard. Gradually, things came together and I've been lucky enough to be able to balance teaching with rehabilitation and treatment.

Do you work with students on classical as well as musical theatre repertoire?

Yes, I feel I know most about musical theatre, as I was a musical theatre performer. However, I've spent years researching and studying the requirements of various singing styles. Doctors refer patients from many disciplines, so I often use language that can be understood by the artist I'm working with.

How would you describe the vocal requirements for singers in musical theatre today? How have those requirements changed over the years and where do you think they're going?

The field has changed so much since my time. In the sixties, we were separated into two categories in auditions: dancers who sang or singers who danced. If you were lucky, you got to sing sixteen bars of an uptempo and possibly a ballad. The standard questions were, "Can you belt?" and "Can you sing legit?" and the gold standard for belting was sounding like Ethel Merman.

Today, you may be singing Millie in *Thoroughly Modern Millie* one day and Maria in *West Side Story* the next. Besides this, we have a new generation of composers who mix styles that are extremely demanding vocally. One character may have to produce a "pop" belt sound, which I differentiate from a musical theatre belt sound, as well as producing high Cs over heavy orchestration with sustained classical lines, for example *Dracula*.

A healthy singer should be able to move from one style of music to another. For that reason, all of my pop singers dabble in art songs and all of my opera singers can belt. By the way, most of these singers can dance and are certainly called upon to do so. Where things will evolve in the next generation is anyone's guess, but it certainly won't get easier.

What is your passion in this work?

It's extremely exciting to work with someone who's had a problem, to fix it, make sure they can sustain it, and then carry it through to the end of a performance. It's like the pretest and retest. Being on the team and following this group of very complex people is extremely fulfilling. That's the upside. The downside is that you're always on call, 24/7. However, most people try to respect my privacy.

One of my favorite things to do takes place in the summer at Ann Reinking's Broadway Theater Project in Florida. For the past six summers, musical director Rob Fisher and I have conducted workshops, taught, and coached the most talented group of young performers imaginable! Rob and I look at things from different perspectives—he as a conductor and I as a technician. It's amazing how these two areas complement each other; it's just a question of which door to open first.

What role does voice science, or vocal anatomy and physiology, play in your work?

It informs everything I do. How much I *communicate* all of this information to them is another question. When I begin work with students, I give them general information on anatomy and physiology. It is essential that they understand support from both a breathing and a postural aspect. However, since we work in so many styles, it is necessary for us to develop a language, or a "recipe," for each style. [Each style] is very specific in terms of laryngeal height, tongue elevation, pharyngeal width, palatal control, and so on.

Does movement or movement-based training play a role in your teaching?

Yes. If you look around this room, you can see physio balls, four- and five-inch balls, therabands, zafus, weights, exercise mats, and the like. I actually started out as a dancer. No one ever told me the reason I could turn one day or fall on my face the next or how come I could raise my leg this much on one side and not the other. When I started working in voice, I was determined that people would not sing with their fingers crossed as I had danced my whole life, and I found that the better the body was organized, the better the sound. This is particularly true since the majority of my clients are people with problems. I work very closely with an osteopath and have learned a great deal about structure, movement and function of the jaw, neck, diaphragm, head, legs, and so on. I'm a great advocate of Pilates, Gyrotonics, yoga, and most recently have been working with Catherine Fitzmaurice on inducing tremors to facilitate freedom. I would be neglectful not to mention Jo Estill, to whom I will always be grateful for the years of work we did together. She is responsible for opening my eyes and mind to the many possibilities that the human instrument is capable of.

Do you teach microphone techniques?

I don't do lots of it because I don't have a sound system in here, but we do talk about it. We talk about placement of mikes. We talk about ear molds and different types of microphones, particularly when people are recording or doing a cabaret at the piano.

THE TRAINING

Where do you start? What are the foundational aspects of training to which you regularly attend?

What I ask people to do first, is to show me how they warm up. Sometimes the warm-up looks just fine but conversely there are times when I can't understand what they are trying to achieve. When I hear that students need forty-five minutes to warm up, an alarm goes off; they should be able to do it in ten or fifteen minutes. At this point, I'm observing support in terms of posture and breath management, looking at their jaw, tongue, laryngeal position, tension in strap muscles, where their head is placed in relation to their spine, what's going on in their feet as well as their pelvis. Occasionally, I may use my hands to shift their posture in one way or another. I might engage them in various activities; for example, holding a chair over their head, draping them over a ball, having them slide down walls, or walk backwards to achieve a more connected and free-flowing sound.

Next, I hear them sing a piece of material, at which time I try to tweak little things and make small suggestions. However, I'm still gaining information; I'm finding out about their resonators, their articulators, and how the breath is managed (too much or too little). Are they straining or pressing to make sound? How efficiently are they working? Will they sustain vocal injuries or do they understand the "margin of safety" within the medium they are performing in? How efficient is their soft palate and are they able to access different types of sounds moving from piano to forte, messa di voce, belt, legit, and so on?

It's at this point that I begin to give some verbal information. The first thing I do is to tell them what they did well, as most of the people I see are really good singers. Then I back them up and introduce a bit of basic anatomy and physiology. Contrary to what people may believe, singers love information and love to draw their own conclusions. Although everyone is different, if the larynx is normal I begin with postural work, emphasizing the relationship between posture and breath management.

People are often surprised that something as slight as a neck and head position can affect their sound. Based on the work that I did with Jo Estill, I begin work on the "two-box model" with an emphasis on where effort is acceptable as opposed to where it is not. I might do some "jump starts" at this point, that include humming, trilling, or singing through straws. During these maneuvers, they can achieve instant success avoiding supra-glottal tensions, and to that we then add a whole series of tools and tricks, culminating in various warm-ups and cool-downs.

I have trained a wonderful group of teaching assistants and they work in a similar manner. We begin with a series called the "Basic Seven," which is a program I have developed to explain various principles of singing, and then we move on from there. The first goal is, of course, to sustain a well-produced tone throughout the registers.

What do you expect to observe in a singer who is well trained or in a performer who sings well, with or without training?

What I expect to observe is that I'm moved, that there's some connection to their heart. I really don't want to see their technique. Sometimes we get so technical that we just take away a singer's individuality and everything becomes generic. I have to confess that every now and then when I feel a singer is "almost dangerous"—for example, Edith Piaf or someone like that—I am moved more than I can imagine. However, I do want to know that they aren't going to kill themselves, because they are going to have to duplicate this in performance many times. So I'm looking for ease, and a sound that they can reproduce, one that is resonant, and doesn't make me nervous to listen to. In other words, I don't want to spend my time worrying about them.

I've often said to people, "I can turn the sound off on my television when somebody is singing and know that I'm going to be either miserable or happy, without even hearing their voice."

Granted, the journey is different from one singer to another, but if you think it appropriate, would you cite a couple of examples of how students might get from their first lessons with you to a solid professional technique?

I think that trust in a teacher is essential. If students decide to work with a particular teacher, they must follow the path that is outlined for them. I spend so much time on vocal hygiene; I can't tell you the things that are taken for granted. It's important that they understand simple things like, "Why are we hydrating? What are the different ways that we hydrate? What's humidification about? What's being slippery about? What foods can you eat? What are warning signals? What are the effects of certain medications on the voice?"

Technique should be based on a series of exercises that involve all of the muscle groups involved in singing (i.e., abduction/adduction, lengthening/shortening). In addition, different layers of the vocal folds must be exercised. In other words, we're building skills and exercising the whole instrument. Many teachers work registers separately and are very successful. However, I don't work in this manner. So my first goal is to even out the voice from bottom to top. I want people to be able to isolate the various parts of their instrument to create different qualities of sound. In other words, to learn a few "recipes."

It's important to me that singers understand their speaking voice and how it relates to singing, how we can vary it, and to understand the differences between opera, musical theatre, jazz, and pop. This is what we do first and we continue from there.

I feel it's important to incorporate repertoire quickly and to eliminate fear. Musical theatre people have to work on material that stretches them in their soprano or tenor range while working on material that "shows them off" in different ways. Finally, they must audition, audition, audition and, hopefully, perform, perform, perform.

In the answers to earlier questions, you have touched on some, if not all, of the six aspects of training listed below:

Alignment, Breathing, Range, Resonance, Articulation, Connection (the Acting Dimension)

Now, from the perspective of your own approach, will you comment specifically on each of these elements, to whatever extent and in whatever order you choose?

Alignment. You can't separate breathing from alignment. It's one and the same. If the body is prepared and organized, the breath will flow. Finding out how to control that breath is important as well; holding breath is as troublesome as forcing too much air out at one time. Therefore, it's important to understand the function of the diaphragm, its relationship to the ribs in inspiration as well as exhalation, and the use of the abdominal muscles. I take people through many postures to achieve this goal.

Range. We develop range, hopefully, immediately. After almost thirty years, I have to say that if they're going to have it, it's going to happen right away. I'm not talking about finesse, but the notes should be there. If the singer is a heavy belter and can still sing high Cs, that's great.

Resonance. I talk about resonance, ring, and tonal energy. I borrow techniques from resonant voice therapy, as well as from the work of Arthur Lessac, Joe Stemple, Kittie Verdolini, and Kristin Linklater. No matter what technique I use, I always stress that there should be a sensation of "buzzing" on the bony structures of the face without any effort at the level of the larynx. Getting different tones to line up, so that the back vowels line up with the front vowels, is sometimes problematic. As early as 1980, I was talking about resonance and achieving greater amplitudes of sound with less breath and less effort. There are so many doors to open and pathways one can follow.

Articulation. I'm a stickler. I spend as much time talking about consonants as I do vowels. In vowel production, I want students to understand the difference between front and back vowels and how they are produced in terms of tongue position in the oral cavity, as well as lip position and mouth opening. However, I also want them to know that if their tongue were really relaxed, they would be able to produce these sounds properly and without thought. Consonants are a little bit trickier. There are many schools of thought about what to do with consonants. Jo Estill cites three solutions to the problem of consonant constriction: (1) Ignore them and sing only vowels; (2) elide them (the clothespin technique); or (3) exaggerate the constriction, recoil to the vowel, and breathe on consonants (Jo's technique). I use the standard classification of consonants in terms of voicing, manner, and place of articulation, and employ various tools for improvement in intelligibility, as well as sound. I've recently begun talking about Arthur Lessac's *Consonant Orchestra*, and using his classifications in comparing consonants to various instruments in the orchestra: sustainable, tappable, and sound effects.

Consonants carry meaning, and if we were to examine the way we talk, we'd find they usually take the emphasis. The ultimate goal is to get students to use the tip and back of their tongue, the hard and soft palate, and lips and teeth without interference from the "pesky jaw."

Connection (the acting dimension). There's no performance without this. Sometimes I take people away from technique and give them an acting assignment and lo and behold they find they're articulating better and their technique is better as well. Various techniques include hand gestures for every word, card tricks, walking and changing directions after every thought. These are ways of opening doors so that students become aware that: (1) Their breath is freer; (2) the material is easier; (3) there is no fear of high notes; (4) they are able to move from belt to mix voice; and (5) the experience is much more rewarding. Conversely, I've worked with actors who say, "I can't think about all that technique; I have to act." What they don't realize is that if they are free, they will have more choice and will ultimately be more exciting. I know that when I'm moved to tears, everything is connected.

Again, from your perspective, how do these individual aspects of training relate to one another (1) in the learning process and (2) in performance?

Let's go backwards; let's go to performance. You've got to have technique working on a subconscious level by this point. Hopefully, you've developed your instrument and it's in good working order. Every performer needs to know what works for him or her. I often give people several warm-ups so they don't get stuck in a particular muscle pattern. However, knowing what warms you up, what to do on a two-show day (Do you lie down and sleep? Do you eat and talk?) is essential. Everybody's a little different. The bottom line is that you must develop a solid routine that works for you (i.e., warming up and cooling down). Understanding "danger" signals and the ability to pull yourself out of a bad situation is essential.

Do you have any additional comments you'd like to make?

It's been a pleasure talking with you. I think teachers are becoming more informed, there is more uniformity in approach and less "voodoo." I can remember one of my first voice teachers who had me blow into the mouthpiece of a trumpet in the name of "technique." She had one eye and a bunch of dogs sitting on benches in a circle who would howl after every sound that came out of my mouth. I'm glad that we're moving away from this sort of thing but, conversely, I don't want students to get too bogged down and lose the sense of art.

So there has to be a balance.

There's room for everything, especially in the world we're living in today. It is our duty to foster and nurture the next generation of performers.

References

Jo Estill, www.evts.com.

Catherine Fitzmaurice, www.fitzmauricevoice.com.

Arthur Lessac, www.Lessacinstitute.com.

4. JEANNETTE LoVETRI

By early afternoon it was wet and blustery on New York's Upper West Side. Still, I managed to find Jeanie LoVetri's apartment quite easily and arrived a few minutes before 2:00. She welcomed me graciously and made tea as we caught up a bit. Then we sat in her living room, thoroughly enjoying the exploration of topics that were dear to both of our hearts. I'd known Jeanie from voice conferences in Miami, New York, and Philadelphia, and had attended her first Contemporary Commercial Music Vocal Pedagogy Institute at Shenandoah Conservatory in Virginia.

Photography by James Kreigsman

Jeannette LoVetri is a past president of the New York Singing Teachers' Association, a member of the National Association of Teachers of Singing, and secretary of the American Academy of Teachers of Singing. Her students can be heard in leading roles on Broadway and in national tours, as well as on network television, in film, and in major concert halls. In addition to her work with singers, Ms. LoVetri has published major articles in the field of voice science, and, in 1999, she was awarded the prestigious Van Lawrence Fellowship by the Voice Foundation for her significant contributions to voice science in the teaching of singing.

PERSPECTIVE

Will you say something about your background and about what influenced or informed your approach to teaching?

I started studying voice when I was fourteen or fifteen, with the local teacher who was in my town. Then I went to Manhattan School of Music, where I did not graduate, and where I was miserable, and after that I basically pursued private training. Then in 1978, I bumped into the Voice Foundation and I started attending the meetings when they were here in New York. I got very interested in vocal production and voice science through that. I continued to read and study on my own and experiment a lot with my own singing, and with teaching and with my students. Eventually, in 1989, Dr. Sataloff asked me to be on the faculty at Voice Foundation, and that's how I got to meet Dr. Johan Sundberg.

And you worked with Dr. Sundberg in Stockholm.

Yes, I went to Stockholm to work with him in 1990, and that's where they studied my throat in different positions and sounds. And we worked with the late Dr. Patricia Gramming and with Ninni Elliot (one of the founders of speech pathology in Stockholm and also a singing teacher). So that began my formal private training in voice science. Then, in between, I also did some work with Dr. Daniel Boone; we did two workshops here in New York. I did some research with Dr. Jason Surow and Dr. Peak Woo. The most recent work was a study with Dr. Allison Behrman. I also went out and did some work with Dr. Ingo Titze about three years ago; I spent three days in Utah, where they stuck electrodes in my larynx and wired me for sound, literally, to study vibrato.

I consider that most of my singing training was not very good, and this is a big influence on how I teach, to make sure that what I do is different. I had some very emotionally and psychologically difficult times with my teachers—not the first lady: She was very sweet and generous with me. On the other hand, she didn't teach me much! There were moments in working with a voice teacher that were downright obnoxious, and I wanted very much to find out why don't these people know more? And I still have a lot of anger and resentment toward the profession and how insular it can be and stuck in the past. I tried to let it go, but whenever I see people teaching, and they are saying something to students that

I know doesn't have anything to do with physiologic function or plain common sense, I still get angry. Sometimes that makes me *persona non grata* to my colleagues, but I guess I have to live with that.

No one really knew voice science when I was a student, so I can't fault anyone for that lack, but non-classical singing has been around and has been ignored by classical teachers for a long time, especially for the past fifty years. If I was going to learn about all these things, there was no school to attend, so I had to go seek out the information on my own.

I just carved out a niche, little by little, here and there, and every doctor, every scientist that I met gave me information and was helpful to me and was a mentor of some kind. It made my teaching clearer and more practical. It allowed me to save time and to be more efficient and accurate in what I was asking students to change or to do, and I can't imagine how I would be doing what I do if I hadn't had this exposure and integrated it along the way.

I have also done a lot of psychological and emotional exploration and have done all kinds of bodywork, which has made me more sensitive to my own body and mind, and to the students' feelings and psychological states. I read about learning theory and worked with various kinds of alternative healing. I integrated all of this as well, and now I try to teach from the standpoint of meeting the student's needs, rather than having some outside agenda of my own.

How would you describe the vocal requirements for singers in musical theatre today? How have those requirements changed over the years and where do you think they're going?

A musical theatre singer today needs to be able to sing virtually any style of music. And you must especially be able to handle rock and roll, because that's where the business has gone and is going to continue to go. The shows that they've written recently, like *Jane Eyre*, and some of the other modern works, like *Marie Christine*, have not been commercially successful. They might be artistically successful, but the rock and roll shows are going like gangbusters. So I would say that young Broadway performers need to be able to handle basic rock and roll, but I would also include pop music and traditional Broadway revival material. If you look at the ads in *Backstage*, they ask for everything. "We want a high soprano who can mix and belt and we want a tenor who can sing falsetto and low F." There was an ad last summer that asked for a bass-tenor. What is that?

The people doing the casting very rarely actually know what vocal demands are reasonable, so I would say that the more students can sing in a variety of colors, a variety of tonal qualities, and be adaptable to the styles of the music, the more commercially successful they'll be, but it all has to be done healthfully, or it won't last.

Why do you teach what you teach? What drives you? What is your passion in this work?

I want to be of service. I am here to support and get underneath the people who are singing, so that I empower them to discover all of what the voice can do and be. I am passionate about the uniqueness of each voice, about the vulnerability of singers who sing with an open heart and mind. I am excited to work with creative artists, people willing to look within, meet themselves, and face up to challenges.

For a long time I felt like a lone wolf. There was almost no one who could talk about non-classical singing as a serious topic, one worthy of serious study and examination as a pedagogical discipline, and on its own terms, not as something that was "lesser than" classical singing. That's less true now. There are several people who are recognized nationally or internationally and who share my beliefs, although not necessarily my approaches.

Another thing that fuels me in terms of why I teach what I teach, and the way I teach, is that I truly love singing myself. I love the experience of making the sound and being in the music, and I really have a great desire when I feel that joy, to share it with other people. When I'm singing and I think, "Gosh, this is such a fabulous thing, to be able to have so much fun," then I want to give it to somebody else.

The third thing that has always driven me, and I think this has gotten me into trouble, is I really wanted to change the profession because I felt that the old school attitude of, "Well my dear, I will impart my wisdom to you and if you are lucky, you could maybe sing, but never as well as me," had to go. I like to think that I had a hand in the fact that voice science is now "the thing" in singing teaching. Ten years ago even, I would be talking about this and people would be looking at me like, "What is she thinking?" I even had people say to me, "Why are you interested in all that science? It's so removed from what we do." And I would say, "On the contrary, it needs to inform what we do." And now, of course, everything that goes on in the singing teachers associations is all science, *da da da*, and whaddaya know about dat?

You're already addressing this, but what role does voice science,
or vocal anatomy and physiology, play in your work with students
or clients?

The most important thing for me was understanding the vertical laryngeal position in relationship to vocal quality, and also the changing of the acoustic spectrum in relationship to what the singer would perceive as a tonal quality, and that there's more than one way to achieve a goal from a physiological place that gives you the acoustic output you need. So if you want a brighter sound, you can smile, you can make it more nasal, you can try to make the sound more forward. There are different ways that you can maneuver the tube, so that it would get a little smaller and that would give you the amplification of the frequencies you need to get the desired result.

I rely a lot on my ears, more than anything else. I use my eyes afterwards, as further feedback about the physical production that I can see. I am looking at posture, and for physical comfort. I know what the physiology is supposed to do and how it looks when it does it. We know, for instance, that if the mouth is closed, it affects the acoustic spectrum. Therefore, with that acoustic picture in my mind, I can actually hear that the mouth is closed, but I do look to check, to make sure that what I hear agrees with what I see. A closed mouth could be positive or negative, a choice or a tense spot. If it is a hindrance, the problem could be caused by a tight jaw, a tight tongue (at the base), a tightly raised larynx, lack of kinesthetic awareness of the jaw itself, and several other things. The more information I acquire, the more I can be direct and simple.

I am not interested in forcing students to just get the external result, regardless of what they have to do to get it. I believe you have to get people to the goal in a free and healthy way, no matter how long that takes, and understand that along the way you might want to be able to be "in the moment" and make adjustments as needed. It's good to be able to say, "Ah, I didn't think of that," or "I didn't expect that sound to show up. Now, we can use this," and it could change things in a significant way.

Does movement or movement-based training play a role in your
teaching?

Yes, but I don't generally do anything much with movement in the lesson myself. I encourage students to go and see practitioners, and I do refer people to specific practitioners or methods of all kinds. I have lots of dance training in my background (more than twenty years total in all kinds of styles), I'm very connected to how I move, and I've done a lot of bodywork, but I never wanted to teach any of it. I have also in the studio the big ball, I have shoulder rollers, I have bodywork tools, and some students will use these on their own.

I choose to operate as if the voice were a hologram. I think of the breath and body as being totally reflected in the vocal sound, and the sound itself is affected by every part of the body and how it moves. I work from the spiritual principle that everything is connected to everything else. I've had many experiences that validate this point of view. If I can get the throat to let go and open up, there will be a corresponding release and opening in the body. If the throat muscles let go, the breath can deepen and be freer, and that changes the posture. So many teachers work from the breath up into the voice, but I work from the voice down into the breath. It is more physiologically correct, since the vocal folds control the airflow, but it runs counter to what most people think and have been taught. Often when something shifts or lets go in the throat itself, the person will say, "Wow, I really felt that in," and they name another part of the body. We are both delighted.

Do you use any recording equipment in your studio?

I do have a mike and an amp, but I teach everybody to sing acoustically, even the rock singers. Sometimes they'll bring in a CD track and they'll sing their vocals over it using the mike.

THE TRAINING

Where do you start? What are the vital signs you check right away when a student comes to you? What are the foundational aspects of training to which you regularly attend?

I spend the whole first session just listening, looking, and experimenting. I am seeking evidence of various vocal functions. I evaluate how someone looks, how they sound, how they respond. What's moving, where is it moving, how is it moving? Where would I locate the vibration of the sound, what kind of a sound is it? How much ease is there? How far can the person take the sound, and where does it seem not to go? And how much awareness does the person have of all of that as it's going on? You can have people who are real messed up, but they know they're real messed up. Or others who are messed up and they have no idea that they're messed up. Those are two different paths. You've got to deal with those things totally differently, as the second is usually much harder to address than the first.

I ask a lot questions in the first session, and I really try to listen to what people are telling me to get some sense of "Why did they come here, and what is it that they want?" And if they're regular students busy working doing gigs, they might say, "Gosh, I'm about to go out and do Kate in *Pirates of Penzance* and I really need to get my upper voice in shape." So that's what I work on. If they're beginning students (I don't have too many nonprofessionals now, but when I did), in each of the first four or five sessions I would do some singing and some explaining. I take out my little skeleton and I show them the ribs and I say, "Now your lungs are here and this is what we're moving." I have a *Breathing for Singing* video; sometimes I'll have people watch that. I'm trying to give them the context in which we will work. And then I usually give them a diagnosis at the end and say, "Well, this is what I hear." Then I sketch out a program that lets people do positive work to improve themselves and I also acknowledge what's already there that's good and just has to be maintained. I am honest about what needs work, but I try always to explain that it is just function, and function can be adjusted.

I think, in terms of diagnosing people, it's taken me many, many years to learn how to hear the inner messages. I have that sort of psychic perception in the sound of, "Oh, there's some kind of trauma here." And the person may not even remember what the trauma is, but I can feel that. And I can also sense in the sound where is it not going in the body, where it's stuck.

What do you expect to observe in a singer who is well trained or in a performer who sings well, with or without training?

Good posture. I expect them to stand up in a nice, straight, but not in a rigid way. I want to see low inhalation but I don't really care whether it's low here, there, or there, as long as it's deliberate and comfortable. I want to hear undistorted vowels, consistent vowels. I would expect to see looseness in the face and jaw and no obvious tension in the neck, at least in middle pitches at moderate volumes. I wouldn't mind some physical exertion on very high notes or very loud notes, as long as it is manageable without vocal strain.

I want to hear a vibrato, a spontaneous vibrato that's not, in my opinion, distorted as too fast, too slow, too little, or too much (too big), and a certain amount of sturdiness in the tone, as well as a certain amount of range, at least an octave and a half to two octaves. And a fairly wide dynamic range between pianissimo and fortissimo on seven eighths of the sung pitches. Then I want to know that when they sing whatever music they sing, they actually can experience feeling emotional or expressive while they sing. For theatre performers, I want to know that they are not "making like" they feel, not singing "as if" they were feeling angry, but are actually *being* angry and singing. And if they can't do that, then I might refer them to some sort of outside training in acting. I guess that's all.

That's a lot, and very comprehensive.

That's the menu.

Granted, the journey is different from one singer to another, but if you think it appropriate, would you cite a couple of examples of how students might get from A to B, or from their first lessons with you to a solid professional technique?

Assuming I have an unlimited time frame (which is rarely true with a professional singer), I work with each of the areas I just mentioned, one or two at a time until the student is able to demonstrate control over them without too much conscious effort. In other words, the designated behavior, or behaviors, just show up. I keep going until I feel we have established three-quarters of the functions on my list, as I just stated it. Along the way, when singers are about 50 percent of the way able to do what we've discussed without stress, I would say, "What sort of repertoire do you want to do?" and if it's music theatre, I would either give them some songs myself or send them to a coach. Most likely send them to a coach, because here in New York, you've got to have good material. And again, this was a choice I made, because I am here. I did not deliberately learn every song of every show, because I don't have to. I just stick to very simple songs with my students, the old warhorse songs, until I feel they're doing well enough, and then I say, "Now go to the coach and get some really interesting, different material that's in the right key and suitable for your type."

And then they would work on it with you as well as with the coach.

That's correct. With the professional singers, it's a little different, because they come in with a career, so I don't have to find songs for them, I don't have to find a repertoire. They're coming to me and saying, "I've got to sing with this combo next week and they want me to do this new piece." So that's fun for me because all sorts of material comes through this door.

What if someone brings in something that you think is inappropriate, and wants to do it?

I tell them. "You're not ready to do this song; you can't sing this song." "Well why?" they'll respond. "Because this song requires vocal capacities that you don't yet have, so I don't think you should sing it." Of course, if they have been hired to do it, then I just try to address it and get it to be as good as possible, compromising wherever necessary so that the voice is as protected as possible. Sometimes they have written the material themselves and then can't sing it because it is written in a way they can't execute, and they don't want to change the writing—they want to change the way the voice works! That's tough.

In the answers to earlier questions, you've certainly touched on some, if not all, of the six aspects of training listed below:

Alignment, Breathing, Range, Resonance, Articulation, Connection (the Acting Dimension)

Now from the perspective of your own approach, would you comment specifically on each of these technical elements, to whatever extent and in whatever order you choose?

I think you have to have all of them or you're really not going to be the world's most wonderful singer. But I also know that there are people who sing who don't have them and they have careers. So with everything here, I think there's an element of striving toward having a balance of them all. You also have to understand that it's possible to compromise, and the degree of compromise has to do with just getting the job done in a way that is healthy. So maybe they don't ever really get a great vibrato, or maybe their vowels do sound a little off, or maybe the tone does stay breathy, but they find a quality and production in the voice that's acceptable and that functions. It doesn't get tired, there are no vocal health issues. All the ingredients would then be balanced against the real-world needs of the person you're working with.

You custom-tailor each item on the list to the person, the material, the current conditions. For instance, the *alignment* is necessary and you have to work on *breathing*, in whatever way is suitable. You do some trial and error, experimenting. Is this a big stocky person? He might breathe all the way to his coccyx bone. Is this a small, delicate person? She might breathe more near the solar plexus or the upper abs. It doesn't matter, as long as it meets their criteria and gets the job done.

Range is something I work on toward the end of all the other things. I work a lot in the middle voice, because that's where the mechanics really show up. If you're going to sing chest in your middle voice, you've got to sing differently than if you are singing head in your middle voice. I want to get that established and then, from that standpoint, I will work on range. And almost always, we'll work on developing head register to extend the range up before I work on chest register to extend the range down. Usually that is the sequence. On some rare occasions with a different voice, that might not be, but I'd say that's the rule.

Resonance. Again, in commercial music, it's a non-issue. They're amplified. So the way I work on resonance is, if you find a sound that's particularly resonant, that is, if it just shows up that way, you can say, "Hey, can you hear that? That's a good sign. Can you track into that without fuss?" And I use it as a teaching tool, an awareness place, but I also encourage the students not to get caught up on resonance, because it's more important to focus on the text or the musical goals. And the only time range is a problem is if someone comes in and has been assigned a part that has a note that's higher than they can comfortably go. Then I'm going to work on range with that person much sooner and we have to calibrate the other skills around that.

I don't do too much with *articulation*. I probably should do more than I do. In the music theatre songs I want to hear the ends of the words. I want to understand everything the person is singing, and occasionally I will do something that is spoken text. Usually, though, I integrate some consonants into the vowel exercises, so that articulation gets addressed indirectly. I find that if you have a relatively decent speaker, as the voice gets lighter and comes more forward, it becomes more flexible, which enhances the articulation, and it all improves over time. Again, occasionally if I have a person with a real problem I will send them to a voice or speech coach or a speech pathologist.

The last one is connection, or the acting dimension.

With music theatre folks, the first few times I let them sing a song I let them work in what I would consider a more technical place. Do they breathe properly? If it's not staying in head register when it needs to stay in head, can they do something about that? They have to have the song pretty much nailed down technically. Then I'm going to say, "Who, what, where, why, when?" I might say, "I've got to believe you, but I don't believe you." And, same thing as with movement, I don't teach acting. If it gets to be an issue, I send them to an acting class, coach, or teacher.

Now, with the jazz people, I don't work that way because they don't *act* in a theatrical sense. I ask a lot of questions, like, "What is it that you want to create here? Is there some mood or energy that you're looking for?" I might say, "I'm not getting that. You want this to sound melancholy? Well, I don't get that melancholy or sadness."

I want to be touched or moved. I try to leave myself wide open as a teacher and just be receiving, receiving, always receiving. If a person's singing something that has some kind of emotional meaning and I don't feel a thing, I'm going to say, "Wait a minute. What's going on here?" I don't like to spend too much time on it, though, as then it becomes "acting lessons." I'd rather send them elsewhere.

Something that I feel passionate about—this is probably at the very top of the list—is that a singer must understand registration.

Oh, yes, please talk about that.

You must understand the source before you deal with the filter, meaning you must understand the function of the vocal folds before you understand how the throat and mouth act upon what happens. The cricothyroid and thyroarytenoid muscles (in the larynx) are the driving forces of register change. If you do not understand register function, I don't care what approach you use, you are not going to get to the goal in an authentic way. I am up in arms about that because so much teaching is still based on "change the filter" (that is, change the vowels), and I think it is possible that the source (the vocal folds themselves) can follow the filter over time, but to me, that's the long way to go; it takes too much time and it doesn't always give you the quality that you need.

In classical singing, teachers tend to put registration into a less serious category because of the emphasis on resonance. Therefore, they are often confused about belting as a quality. Belting has been a known entity for generations on Broadway. The people on Broadway who are belters know that they're belting when they're belting. It is just chest register, or the speaking voice quality, carried up above the normal speaking range, and at high volume. If it isn't fairly intense, it isn't belting. That doesn't mean, however, that belters can't sing softly, or in other qualities, or that they have to belt. Those kinds of limitations would indicate poor singing skills or symptoms of vocal dysfunction. I suppose if you've never made a belt sound yourself, you may not be able to identify the sound acoustically in anyone else. So many of the classical people think that any brassy sound is belting! Wrong.

The most fascinating technical place to go is when you are changing registration, or register quality, deliberately. You are really working with very interior, intrinsic musculature and response, and you just can't substitute one register quality for the other as if they were the same. You cannot acoustically substitute a juiced-up head register sound for a mixy (part chest, part head) sound. Think how dumb opera singers sound when they try to sing pop music. There are reasons why it never works, and they are registration reasons.

Head register is a different sensation than chest; it produces a different response in the vocal folds, in the larynx, in the airflow and in the use of the physical apparatus. It is not just a *stylistic* difference. I do get on the soapbox here and stomp up and down and scream and yell. If you don't understand register function, then in my opinion, nothing else is going to work right.

You *cannot* work on registration through breathing, through posture, through resonance or through nasality, even though all of these things will change the sound in some way. You can change the posture, the breathing patterns in the body, the vowel sound shape, and even the range of pitches sung, and still not change registration. If this point is not understood, you can waste a lot of time and never really get anywhere. It is not something that can be ignored by anyone who wants to sing or teach non-classical singing in any style.

*And you're talking about understanding mentally, physically, and
every other way possible.*

I am. I'm talking about when you are singing in your lower register, you
are going to more easily access anger and powerful sadness and be in contact with your primary emotions. When you're singing a head register
sound, it's much easier to find vulnerability and delicacy and grace and
purity. You need both. Registration anchors the emotions. If you want me
to sound pure and sweet and I don't have a head register, I'm going to have
a tough time, unless I can make a breathy chest register. So the registers·
also function as doorways into the feelings.

This is a concept I haven't heard before, Jeanie.

I'll give you a good example of this, Joan. Frank Wildhorn's *Jekyll and Hyde*
is pop music. He writes formulaic songs, and everything is done full out,
and for the women the music is commonly very high and very belty. If you
closed your eyes, and you didn't understand the meaning of the English
words, you would never have known what emotions the singers were expe-
riencing because there was no quality change. It was just, Let's sing loud
for loud's sake; let's belt in this quality for volume's sake alone. We definitely know that this person is upset, but we don't know whether she's
upset because she's sad, because she's frightened, or because·she's angry.
You cannot tell, because the choice is: I have to belt this sound and it
has to be loud.

*So there's no real connection with the text. It's all about belting
and being loud.*

I think so. I think a lot of times the singers get caught up in the. volume
and the intensity of the sound for its own sake. They live in the volume,
and then, yes, they are feeling their feelings, but it's so over the top that
you can't hear it.

I was part of a study that Mount Sinai was doing on the effect of theatrical smoke on actors' voices. I had to see *Beauty and the Beast* in order to
know what was going on. They couldn't give me a ticket, so they stuck me
in the sound booth with the sound guy. And I watched him run the sound-
board during the show. Fascinating. This huge, big board, and they're
singing and he is moving knobs up and down with both hands all through

every song. I thought they set a level and left it that way. So at intermission I said, "Can I ask you some questions?" He said, "Sure." I said, "Are you changing the sound on every line of every single song?" He said, "Yeah." I said, "Why are you doing that?" "Well," he said, "you know, they sing differently every day, and I have to adjust. Of course, when they're face to face, I have to turn one mike off while the other person's singing. I have to adjust the mikes on and off throughout the song." "Really?" I said, "I only know a little bit about this stuff. Did I really see 90–95 decibels on your sound meter?" He said, "No, it's 110. That's what the orchestra is set at." I said, "My god, that's like a jet engine!" He said, "I know. We keep it that high because the producers like it loud; they find it more exciting. And when we take it down and they come back, they yell at us and we have to put it back up. On opening night it was 115 decibels." That is the threshold of pain. Now this is in the Palace Theatre, an acoustic house that was built for vaudeville, with unamplified voices. Why are the producers requiring this? Because they don't know music, don't know singing, don't know acting, don't understand the voice, and don't know what else to evaluate except volume. If it's loud, it's great! No, it's pathetic.

This also has an impact on what we teach, because if you teach singers to feel real emotions and express real feelings, it isn't necessarily going to be validated by the people who have the power to give them work. The singer may go to an audition and somebody could say: "That's great, but can you take it up a third higher and do it louder?" "Well, no." "Next." What would you do, as a young performer trying to get a job? Please the person and get the job or take care of yourself and maybe be out of work? We have gotten used to using volume as a shortcut to emotional stimulation. Some people can get away with it better than others in terms of vocal health. But that's also one of the reasons I harp all the time, come back to registers, because a lot of times that's the name of the game. If you don't get the correct register quality and connect that to something in terms of emotions, you're sunk both physically *and* emotionally. This situation isn't going to change in the near future, either.

Again, from your perspective, how do these individual aspects of training relate to one another (1) in the learning process and (2) in performance?

Well, you can't be emotionally open if you don't breathe. So another connection to register function is that the larynx needs to be loose enough and strong enough to receive a full exhale. The breath needs to be able to just go wherever it goes, if you really just let go and let the sound out. And it's difficult to do that if your middle voice is not coordinated. When the larynx is relaxed and comfortable, but also vital and energized, it should be possible for the person to take a deep, easy, free inhalation and be comfortable on an exhalation, even a vigorous exhalation. The breathing can't easily happen if the postural alignment is bad, so you cannot get a good deep breath if you can't stand up straight in a comfortable way. You really aren't going to have resonance if your throat is tight, and you can't get much range if your mechanism is stiff. So, to me, it's like spokes on a wheel: Sooner or later you've got to address everything, and one thing helps or hinders the others. That's why you can always get there; any road will take you to Rome, provided the teacher has the right intention, which is to serve the needs of the student, and provided he or she understands vocal function from a physiologic place and knows the correct parameters of the style of music the singer is performing. Now I do think that some paths are shorter than others. And when you're looking to expand the process, I always think of it as a globe getting bigger, so that students continuously get more aware of their body, more aware of their breathing, more aware of their ability to ride on the breath and connect to the body in a fluid way. More able to allow the sound to go out in all kinds of ways, but still feel like they have control over it as it comes out.

I really believe that if you don't like your own sound, you're not going to get up and sing without some kind of emotional discomfort, and that comes across to the listener. If you've been programmed by some voice teacher that the "right" way to sing is X way, and X doesn't really feel comfortable or sound authentic, but you do it anyway because you have been convinced, you're always going to have that little place inside that feels disconnected from your own authentic core. If you're really a singer, if you were born to sing, that's a very sad place, because it keeps you out of touch with your heart and with your desire to sing joyfully. I've had singers in here who've sounded spectacular. I mean, you would just say, "Wow!" if you were listening only to the sound for its acoustic output. But if you learn to listen more intuitively, more deeply, you can sense that sometimes the sound, the singing, isn't coming from a place that is really their own voice. It's something that they were either attracted to, or attached themselves to, or someone in authority had told them they ought to do, and they haven't met the challenge in themselves as an artist to ask themselves the crucial questions, "What is my real voice? Who am I vocally?"

Do you have additional comments you'd like to make about your work, singing?

I never expected to be where I am.

But you've allowed yourself to grow however you were meant to grow.

Well, I hope so. I feel that my path has been one of breaking the old paradigms, out in front of the pack changing things, and, again, I don't think that was a deliberate intention. When I was a kid I don't remember thinking, "Oh, I'm going learn to sing all these different sounds and then go tell others what it's like to make them." I am astounded that I'm now teaching in an institute that was created for my work at Shenandoah Conservatory and that it's growing and getting bigger each year.

I think the world needs this book, Joan, for people to see that there are many different approaches and that, ultimately, if the teacher's heart is in the right place, it can work. And voice teachers need to see that you can't just go learn voice science and then that's some kind of magic. You have to find a way to make it make sense, and not just spout the names of muscles. So I think it will be interesting to see where singing training goes, and wherever it unfolds, what it will be like by the time we're old codgers, how much more we'll know.

I'm not sure where the music business is going, but I think it will continue to diversify, to be influenced by world music. I think singers will continue to be asked to sing more and more styles of music in more and more athletic ways. I don't think anybody who's involved in teaching likes all of the artistic products that we see. I think it's true in Broadway, I think it is true in dancing, in film, in recordings, even in fine art. Commercialism—what sells—rules all. The people making the decisions are money people so that the artistic product has less and less validity. There's nothing we can do about that unless our society changes.

Overall that doesn't seem to be happening.

Not right now.

PUBLICATIONS

——. "Female Chest Voice." *Journal of Singing*, Vol. 60, No. 2; (November/December 2003): 161–164.

LoVetri, J. L. "Who's Minding the Store?" *Journal of Singing*, Vol. 59 No. 4; (March/April 2003): 345–346.

——. "Contemporary Commercial Music (CCM) Survey: Who's Teaching What in Non-classical Music." *Journal of Voice*, Vol. 17, No. 2 (2003): 207–216.

LoVetri, J. L., & Weekly, E. M. "Contemporary Commercial Music: More than One Way to Use the Vocal Tract." *Journal of Singing*, Vol. 58, No. 2; (January/February 2002): 249–252.

Surow, J. B., & LoVetri, J. L. " 'Alternative Medical Therapy' Use among Singers: Prevalence and Implications for the Medical Care of the Singer." *Journal of Voice*, Vol. 14, No. 3 (2000): 398–409.

Surow, J. B., LoVetri, J. L., Lesh, S., & Woo, P. "Preliminary Study on the Ability of Trained Singers to Control the Intrinsic and Extrinsic Laryngeal Musculature." *Journal of Voice*, Vol. 13, no. 2 (1999): 219–226.

Sundberg, J., Gramming, P., & LoVetri, J. "Comparisons of Pharynx, Source, Formant, and Pressure Characteristics in Operatic and Musical Theatre Singing." *Journal of Voice*, Vol. 7, No. 4 (1993): 301–310.

Titze, I., Story, B., Smith, M., & Long, R. 2002. "A Reflex Resonance Model of Vocal Vibrato." *Journal of the Acoustical Society of America*, 111(5): 2272–2282. J. LoVetri Research Associate.

Web site: www.thevoiceworkshop.com

5. Mary Saunders-Barton

Photography by Molly O'Mara

Sounds of "Quando men vo" reached us from the studio down the hall as we sat at the kitchen table. Singers came in and out of the room to get water and make brief conversation. I hadn't seen Mary since the spring before, when she'd done several workshops for my students in California. Yet her approach, her positive energy, and her very special presence had played a role in virtually every lesson I'd taught since then.

Mary Saunders-Barton is a gifted teacher. Her work is direct, positive, encouraging, honest, and clear, and she is a specialist in musical theatre. Mary is head of voice instruction for the bachelor of fine arts program in musical theatre at Penn State University and maintains a studio for professional singers in Manhattan. She is an active performer with Broadway, off-Broadway, film, and television credits, and has recently concentrated on the creation and performance of one-woman cabaret shows, the first of which, Stop, Time, *played to sell-out houses in New York. Mary is a frequent presenter at major voice symposia in the United States and abroad, and has been a featured clinician at National Association of Teachers of Singing (NATS) conferences in New York, San Diego, New Orleans, Vancouver, and Minneapolis.*

I. Perspective

*Will you say something about your background and about what
influenced or informed your approach to teaching?*

My initial academic background was in French and French literature.
My own voice training began classically, studying French art song with
Pierre Bernac in Paris during graduate school at the Sorbonne, and then
ranging through a variety of classically oriented teachers in New York
City. Marge Rivingston was my only musical theatre voice teacher, in
the seventies. And my first job following graduate school was not in the
theatre; it was teaching French at a private school in New York. But I was-
n't happy teaching French, so I began studying acting at HB Studios, the
Greenwich Village school developed by Herbert Berghof and Uta Hagen.
Aaron Frankel, author of *Writing the Broadway Musical*, was my first
instructor at HB, and he remains a dear friend and mentor. With beginner's luck, I landed my first acting job at my first audition. I went to an
audition for a production of *Camelot* I saw advertised in *Backstage*. In retro-
spect, I see how remarkably lucky I was, but at the time I just had an
overwhelming feeling of rightness, that I had stumbled into a real calling.
I remember thinking, "I'm home, I'm home." I ultimately did Guenevere
five times. I was right for the Lerner and Loewe leading ladies; I also played
Eliza Doolittle and Gigi. After I'd acted for a few years, I started teaching
voice on the side, the way people sometimes do, coaching friends for auditions. Pretty soon I was making some serious money so I started taking
what I was doing more seriously. Then I got pregnant, had babies, and
suddenly I was teaching pretty much full time. Ultimately, I studied with
lots of different voice teachers and I learned something different from each
one. One pivotal moment of insight came for me when a classical teacher
said (now, this is a classical remark, this whole idea of Fach), "You're not
a soprano; you're a mezzo," so suddenly I realized something about the
way vocal issues are perceived classically, and I sensed that musical theatre
singing was diverging from the classical model. Nobody in musical theatre
wants to think, "Oh, gee, I'm a mezzo. I guess I won't be singing any
ingénue roles." I say now that *every* musical theatre singer has to sing
everything. We don't have the luxury of Fach. So I'm a mezzo *and* I'm
a soprano. But what you notice about musical theatre women is the
strong middle, because the voice has to be put together there, blended

there. You don't have the luxury of saying, "Oh I'll just sing from a
G up" or "I'll just sing the low notes." This is new; it has changed during
my tenure as a teacher in New York City. The old audition ads in the
trade papers called for separated voices—"We want sopranos; we want
altos who belt"—because the concept was that belting was chest voice. But
it's a mix. And now, of course, every soprano belts and every soprano sings
high as well.

*Do you work with students on classical as well as musical theatre
repertoire? Do you teach vocal styles other than classical and/or
musical theatre?*

My Penn State students are required to work on classical repertoire
because, as I said, musical theatre voices these days have to cover all
bases. I teach classical music, because philosophically the two can't be
separated, though acting is the top priority in musical theatre while the
music trumps everything in classical singing. But for the most part
I would say I am a musical theatre specialist. I don't presume to teach
jazz styling, except insofar as it applies to musical theatre singing.
I mean, if somebody is in *City of Angels*, you've got to have some idea
what that's about, the kind of mobility required. And I can help a student cope with *Rent* or a revival of *Hair*, but I certainly don't teach rock
style as a matter of course. I would never call myself a classical teacher,
even though I have certainly sung classically. I've done a few operas that
were very light, and I love classical singing, but I don't call myself a classical singer or teacher. I have several colleagues at Penn State who are
expert in classical singing and we communicate quite freely and openly.
When I first got to Penn State, musical theatre was a fledgling program
in the school of theatre. The students had to trek into the music building for their singing lessons in studios where they were preceded and
followed by classical vocal performance majors working on Schubert or
Verdi. So they felt like the "nonsingers." They never wanted to get up
and sing in front of the vocal performance majors because they were
intimidated. They thought, "Gee, we don't *really* sing." Well, that had
to change and has. I am mighty proud to say that has *so* changed. The
musical theatre students perform regularly in a weekly forum with the
classical vocal majors. They sing Schubert; they sing Sondheim. I think
it's been very positive for everyone.

How would you describe the vocal requirements for singers in musical theatre today? How have those requirements changed over the years and where do you think they're going?

They are constantly changing. It's like riding a wild horse right now; just stay with it. So what's the future holding? Obviously, I don't have a crystal ball, but I do see that everybody's singing higher. The music is edgier, more risky, because that makes it more exciting to the audience, and pushing boundaries becomes the absolute order of the day. That applies to men as well as women, and it's changed my teaching in the past year or two. I'm starting to see the similarities more and more. At the passaggio, you have the potential for what we call *belt* in women's voices. At the passaggio in men, you also have the potential for that same thing, or for something very similar, and it occurs around F#/G, just as in women it occurs around F#/G. It's interesting that there's such a specific parallel. Whether we call it belting or not, men have this option at the top, where they can go into a traditional mixed quality with slightly lower laryngeal position or into a speaking quality where the larynx stays at speech level; raise the soft palate, uncovered tone comes out, and suddenly you get this incredibly bright sound—and I've seen this time and time again—they think it's very exciting, just as the women do when they begin belting. "Oh, we can make the same kind of sound because of the same ingredients!" There they are— bright, high, forward, spoken. If you listen to and compare what Hugh Jackman did with "Oh, What a Beautiful Morning" to the original by Alfred Drake, you'll hear a striking example of what I'm talking about. So for men and women the future is demanding: They have to be able to access all vocal options. For musical theatre it is no longer either/or; it is all-inclusive. All boys are bari-tenors; all girls are sopranos who belt.

Why do you teach what you teach? What drives you? What is your passion in this work?

I am the biggest nerd. A voice nerd. A musical nerd. It's hideous now because I don't even know what a busman's holiday is, because I am *always* on that same holiday. I'm a nerd, but then I think you are, too.

Yes, I am.

My husband is a little over this, although he really loves it too, but he'd kind of like to change the subject now and then. We fell in love on stage doing *My Fair Lady* and, you asked what my passion is—I don't think I've ever lost that feeling. As long as I can keep doing this—singing, teaching singing—I'll just stay in love. And what drives me? Joy—my students' and my own. These young students can be held back by a false sense of limitation. They can't fall back on long experience to give them confidence. But why do I teach what I teach? Because they *do* get it. They find that commitment and that release into circumstance, into character, into acting, and I guess it's life-changing for young people. It's liberating for me as a teacher. Constantly I reexperience the joy of that discovery and release, and who could not love that, being in a situation where you are constantly discovering more about yourself? It's a wonderful job.

Yes, it is! What role does voice science, or vocal anatomy and physiology, play in your work?

I am no scientist. I always work from the point of view of sensation and resonance. I don't discuss, for the most part, laryngeal position, but I listen carefully to my colleagues who are informed. So I'm a vocalist, not a scientist. Over the years I have become my own lab. "Can I do this? How does this feel? Can I do that? Does it feel liberating? Can I make these sounds? How do they feel to me? Do they feel open and free and like I'm just expressing myself in a very natural way, or do they feel costly?" The students I teach in New York are working actors and the kids I teach at Penn State certainly hope to be. I don't feel that my first responsibility is to explain the thyroarytenoids or the cricothyroids, although I'm interested. But when I talk about those things, I try to use dramatic imagery. I would use a nonscientific approach. I might say, "You've gone to the circus and you've seen these lovely ladies standing on the two dappled gray horses, straddling two horses while they trot beautifully around the ring. And then they pick the foot up effortlessly from one of the horses and put it down behind the other foot and then they're riding one horse—but the other horse is trotting patiently along at the side; that's your thyroarytenoid. I've decided I'm going to be in head voice, and how gracefully I did it. You didn't even notice I switched. And then I come back into the mixed voice, back to riding two horses . . . and he's magically there. But you have to keep them coordinated because if they separate you'll fall in the break. So the key is coordination, because you need to be able to communicate directly with both of those elements all the time. They have to be interchangeably used. As I said, I'm no scientist. I talk to them about sensation, imagery.

Do you use any recording equipment in your studio? Do you teach microphone techniques?

I don't teach microphone technique. I think of that as a recording studio issue more important to pop singers than stage performers. Broadway stages are all amplified these days and smart performers can no doubt adjust and let the mike do things for them. But this is all I can tell you about what I encourage: Use your voice and let them deal with it, the sound techies. Use your voice the way you would use it doing eight non-amplified shows a week. Then, if you are amplified, you can make careful adjustments.

II. THE TRAINING

Where do you start? What are the foundational aspects of training to which you regularly attend?

I attend to exactly the same things that any classical teacher would, absolutely all those issues about breathing and alignment. The first thing I attend to that a classical teacher might or might *not* attend to is the speaking voice. In musical theatre we can't afford to have that disconnect. So from day one, literally as they walk in the door, I'm listening to them speak, and I tell them that. I may say to a girl, "Okay, your voice is pitched way too low because it's way out of the range that we're going to be singing. You're talking around a low B below middle C, and they do not sound alike—your speaking and your singing voice. So here you are, you're eighteen years old; let's get a little life in that sound, more buoyancy; then you're going to feel that in your speech." Where the speaking voice travels, that singing voice will travel. And I'm starting to encourage them to think of the upper extension as speech, too. I know you do that.

Yes, of course.

But then, having said that, we don't speak this way in the middle [demonstrates without any chest quality], because it doesn't have feet. So we do have to adapt.

I like what you just said: "It doesn't have feet."

My voice teachers: "Hello Mary, how are you [speaking in an operatic sound]?" So we've got to get that thyroarytenoid working. The issue I encounter with getting that thyroarytenoid involved is the impulse to shift out of it (you know, if you're riding the horses) and to step off and just be on the one around B above middle C. Once that is dealt with and you don't let yourself "lift" too soon, the voice achieves a kind of natural balance and moves right up in speech. The bravest thing I ever said, back when I was starting, when I didn't have the nerve to say anything independent, I started saying, "Okay, guys, delay the passaggio. Just don't give in to it then." Then the problem further up is not anywhere near as great. You must learn not to carry too much weight as you go up. Weight meaning chest. You don't want too much woofer when you're headed for tweeter. That's what a shriek is, a very healthy shriek. So, high F#/G? No problem. All the students can do that. They can all belt high As, if they have healthy instruments. Or they can move into head around E flat. The option is always theirs.

I love what you're saying and it clarifies a lot of things.

Some do it easily and some have to work hard to find the right coordination in the middle so they have parallel options. It's my job not to let them get stuck along the way. I say the voice needs to go on a diet as you go up, because you've got to let some ballast go, or you get this elephant-butt kind of sound that becomes pushed—what classical teachers call a *spread tone*. Most students get it. It takes a while if it is not inherent. With men, there's the tendency to bail out around a high G. It takes commitment and energy to add notes above that in mix, to keep from pushing. For the women, the trouble begins around A flat above middle C, but all men are lyric baritones in this musical theatre context. All girls are mezzos *and* sopranos.

What do you expect to observe in a singer who is well trained or in a performer who sings well, with or without training?

I look for a mixed voice. I look for a centered speaking voice, neither too high nor too low, and the ability—intuitive or trained—to move readily into and out of the mix. I was an intuitive singer because my speaking voice was centered. A well-trained singer, from my standpoint, in terms of doing musical theatre rep, has mobility and flexibility. *Flexibility* meaning change of laryngeal position, use of the musculature, and coordination of those elements. If you have a mixed speaking voice when you walk in the door, you can more or less sing any pop song in the book. If you do not, you cannot. I use as my acid test, [sings] "Did you ever know that you're my hero?" That is incredibly hard for a nonmixed sound. But it's easy for anybody who sings in the middle. I look for the qualities of speech that you would naturally use, extended into the middle singing register. Does it move easily from one range to another? What happens at the very margins, what do you do about those margins (which we like to call *passaggio*), what can you do to build power into the margins, so you don't feel that the net weakens at any point? Those are the things I look for. I absolutely look for a car parked in every garage. You have to have a filled-in voice. You can't trick it. You cannot conceal.

Granted, the journey is different from one singer to another, but would you say something about how students might get from A to B, or from their first lessons with you to a solid professional technique?

Build from the middle, both directions out. Middle up, middle down. I wouldn't have said that ten years ago. I would have said top down, and then I would have said, "And then you kind of bring the bottom up a little." It's not an exact science and it does feel chaotic sometimes, because you're working with muscles you can't directly control, and it is going to be discouraging. It takes time. This is a lifelong journey. So at the university level we just get them as far as we can in the time we have. Some of them really do get to what I would call a professional level by senior year, the musical theatre students, not classical vocal performance. Different. Musical theatre is a young person's art, so they really have to be ready to step out. And you have to get them at least with a good solid middle. Not everybody can do it by the time they graduate, but some of my students—you'd be amazed. They do it better than I do.

In the answers to earlier questions, you have touched on some, if not all, of the six aspects of training listed below:

Alignment, Breathing, Range, Resonance, Articulation, Connection (the Acting Dimension)

Now, from the perspective of your own approach, will you comment specifically on each of these technical elements, to whatever extent and in whatever order you choose?

I work with *resonance*, not with registration. Clearly a great deal of my time in the studio is spent trying to help students create a thoroughly blended voice. *Range* is unlimited. That's one of the lyrics in *Wicked*, "Unlimited." And "Defying Gravity." Isn't that what we're all about? It's a metaphor for itself, for singing. *Breathing*, the Holy Grail of singing. Voice teachers are defined by the way they teach a concept of *free air*. It can be challenging because students come in with such a variety of tensions. I use a combination of imagery and physical movement to help singers move air in and out freely, maintaining the buoyancy of the inhalation on the exhaled tone. I use the term *support* less and less in my teaching because I have found it often results in muscling and pushing. Singing is breathing. Breathing issues are similar for classical and musical theatre singing, with some serious differences. You usually don't have to tap dance while singing a Schubert song or an aria. And some of the students drawn to musical theatre started dance lessons, ballet training, when they were very young and the use of the abdominal muscles and the diaphragm they learned for ballet sometimes presents difficult breathing issues. But, as I said, for the most part the breathing issues faced in the classical studio and the musical theatre studio are similar. Low breath, column of air, open rib cage. But in musical theatre an occasional high breath, an audible breath is not a sin. Any sound a person makes in life may find its place in musical theatre, depending on the emotional demands being placed on the character at the moment, and if the character needs a sobbing intake of breath, or a gasp or an asthmatic wheeze, so be it.

Alignment—we talked about that. *Articulation* is a no-brainer for musical theatre. Every single word must be spoken. Vowel modification? I don't buy it. Not in the theatre. Look, shoot the composer who wrote the climactic note on the /u/ vowel, but do it right. Do the /i/ vowel right. Don't lie to us, because we all hear it. You're faking. The acting dimension? Acting is everything. In musical theatre you have to act, sing, and dance, in that order of priority—acting/singing/dancing—but the singing and dancing skills are at the service of the dramatic imperative. You can have a career without dancing, though good movement is vital. And no matter how fine your voice is, you have to have that acting first. Act, tell the story, or nobody's interested. You will go nowhere.

Again, from your perspective, how do these individual aspects of training relate to one another (1) in the learning process and (2) in performance?

Voice lessons for musical theatre cannot just be about sounds. Synthesis of movement, singing, and acting is vital from the beginning. Every musical theatre teacher is an acting teacher and a movement coach. At any given moment we can stop to isolate and work on one of the specific elements, but too much time spent without returning to the need for synthesis threatens that most important connection to the emotional and physical life of the character.

Do you have additional comments you would like to make?

No, I guess I've talked enough.

PUBLICATION

Saunders-Barton, M. 2005. "The Well-Spoken Singer," in *Shakespeare Around the Globe*. New York: Applause; pp. 281–282.

REFERENCE

Frankel, A. 2000. *Writing the Broadway Musical*. New York: Da Capo.

6. NEIL SEMER

Neil had just done a brilliant work-shop for my students and we were off to LA to see La Bohème. *He was on the West Coast for speaking engage-ments and had students doing major roles in the opera. It was great to see him, and would there be time for an interview? Probably not, so we'd do it by phone.*

Neil Semer was a major presenter — Photography by James Luisi

at the first National Association of Teachers of Singing (NATS) Conference on Belting, in Miami, January of 2000, and the physicality of his approach fascinated me. It seemed so directly related to theatre voice. I've since observed his work with singers from many parts of the world, and in the year following the conference, had the good fortune to study with him briefly in New York.

Neil Semer is a master teacher of voice and gives workshops internationally on the subject of vocal technique and performance practice. His main studio is in New York, and he teaches regularly in Toronto, London, Paris, and through-out Germany. The Neil Semer Summer Vocal Institutes, in Coesfeld and Aub, Germany, are in their eleventh season (2007) and attract participants from major international opera houses, as well as from musical theatre. His teach-ing combines "the old Italian School of Bel Canto, as expounded by Giovanni Battista Lamperti, with scientific understanding of vocal function" (N. Semer, July 9, 2004).

PERSPECTIVE

Will you say something about your background and about what influenced or informed your approach to teaching?

I had a very varied background when I was young. I did "one of everything," which at the time, was a very unfocused kind of performing career. Funnily enough, it turned out to be a very good background for a teaching career. I did classical music, theatre music, pop music, mime, classical theatre, comic theatre, improvisational comedy, among other things. So I got a very broad view of theatre and music and that served me well as I began to teach. I could really understand the different needs of varying kinds of performers. My first real influence of teaching was the book *Vocal Wisdom*, by Giovanni Battista Lamperti. It's a book about the philosophy of singing, to which I then supplemented current understanding of vocal science.

Do you work with students on classical as well as musical theatre repertoire?

Yes, I do, but there's one thing I'd like to say in reference to that question, and that is: I do not teach classical music to non-classical singers. I look for singers to sing from their passion, their own personal sort of musicality, what they are expressive with. I will work on classical repertoire with a classical singer, because that's what they love, and that's what they have a feel for and the direction they want to go. I do not believe in teaching an Italian art song to a person who will never sing in Italian, who has lousy Italian, and who doesn't relate to Italian vocal style. He or she might relate to singing with a really healthy sense of line that one might find in a Rodgers and Hart song, or even a pop tune. I'm looking for people to engage their artistry at the earliest possible moment, and to do that, I think people have to sing music they relate to.

I'm glad you added that, because it's a really interesting perspective. How would you describe the vocal requirements for singers in musical theatre today? How have those requirements changed over the years and where do you think they're going?

Musical theatre is much harder on voices now than it ever used to be. In the old classic musical, forty to eighty years ago, each singer had less to sing.

Leading role singers would sing three or four, at the very most, five songs in a show. Now, some of the musicals that are written, *Miss Saigon*, for instance, are through composed. Therefore, people sing much more in an evening, and sometimes it's music that is much harder on the voice. They are aided with microphones, so if they have good microphone technique and don't push their voices, they can survive it pretty well. However, there is no escaping that people tend to sing more and harder music than was written in prior decades.

It's not going to let up, is it?

I don't think it will get any easier anytime soon, no.

What role does voice science, or vocal anatomy and physiology, play in your work?

It plays a very important role. I think it is any voice teacher's first job, to help make the student aware of the physical nature of the instrument. That's just the beginning of what a good technique is, because it is ultimately more personal than that. But I do believe that all teachers should have a good knowledge of the anatomy of the human body as a whole, vocal anatomy, and acoustics. We need to understand it and be able to communicate it in simple terms to our students.

Does movement or movement-based training (e.g., the Alexander Technique, yoga, Feldenkrais, Pilates) play a role in your teaching?

Certainly Alexander Technique does. The others less so. Pilates is obviously wonderful, but I think it can be a little rigid for singers. Yoga is wonderfully releasing, stretching, and centering, but not specific enough to the act of singing.

THE TRAINING

Where do you start? What are the foundational aspects of training to which you regularly attend?

First, I start on alignment. There's no point in going to other things if good alignment isn't there. Second, I teach what it is to open the vocal tract. Third, I go to breathing. Then I start to deal with connected phonation.

I may use lip trills to start to get the breath moving and coordinate it with vocal utterance. Then I work to develop the musical idea of *line*, of the spinning line I should say, along with the balance of the heavy and light mechanism (thyroarytenoid and cricothyroid muscles). I then do that on vowels. I work on getting the articulation of consonants as agile and as far forward on the tongue tip and lips as possible. In Italian, one says, "*I consonanti sono i fiori dei labbri*," which means "The consonants are the flowers of the lips." So when one experiences the consonants very far forward on the tongue tip and lips, we get the voice, as some people call it, well (or forwardly) placed. I always balance that with a deep position of the larynx and a connected sense of tracheal resonance.

If you are teaching a musical theatre singer, would that be different, for example, from a classical position of the throat?

I don't teach different positions of the throat. I apply what I've already discussed to different repertoire, depending upon the singer I'm working with. But I know there are some musical theatre teachers who teach positioning this way or that way. I am looking for openness, connectedness, and musical and dramatic truth. Style, I believe, is best left to the individuality of the artist. I believe it is my job to work on fundamentals, which allow individual artists to fly on the wings of their own creativity. I teach an open, released larynx, no matter what style I am working with.

What do you expect to observe in a singer who is well trained or in a performer who sings well, with or without training?

I expect to see ease. I expect to feel comfortable that that person can get through the performance and preferably eight performances a week. Ease, connectedness, simple truthfulness, boldness, and spontaneity are all important to me.

Granted, the journey is different from one singer to another, but if you think it appropriate, would you cite a couple of examples of how students might get from A to B, or from their first lessons with you to a solid professional technique?

I give students what is the singing equivalent of a ballet barre. I'm looking for certain physical responses to get automatized, so that singers can be truly in their artistry, in their feeling mode when they're performing. To do that, I give them exercises to automatize alignment, openness in the throat, low breathing, and speech that is clear and agile without tension in the articulators. I will work on their alignment, and just show them exactly how to do it *outside* of singing. I will show them how to open their throat and do it as an athletic act outside of singing. I give them a lot of nonsing-ing exercises, so that in the moment of phonation, the body is already trained to respond in a particular way. So I will work on breathing as breathing. I will work on speaking as speaking, opening as opening, length-ening of the spine as lengthening of the spine, so that when we go into the artistic act of singing a phrase, those things are in some way already start-ing to function without thought or local (read: piecemeal and uncoordi-nated) control.

So the singer is able to work beyond those mechanical things that are already in place.

I seek the whole artistic act, rather than a particular technical point when one sings. Gymnastics to develop the various sorts of local control already mentioned should be done away from singing as much as possible.

In the answers to earlier questions, you have certainly touched on some, if not all, of the six aspects of training listed below:

Alignment, Breathing, Range, Resonance, Articulation, Connection (the Acting Dimension)

Now, from the perspective of your own approach, would you comment specifically on each of these technical elements, to whatever extent and in whatever order you choose?

I start with *alignment*. There are basically three energies in the body. The first is groundedness. So I'm looking for people to feel the floor under their feet, release in their knees, and the pelvis releasing under them. I call those elements that tie us to the earth grounding energy. The second energy I'm looking for is the floating upward sort. One could say, on the metaphysi-cal plane, that it's a spiritual dimension. The spine, the neck and head seem to release, floating upward. The third energy is the energy of the heart. At the level of the sternum, there's a feeling of openness and forward movement, which is metaphysically the opening of the heart to one's public. So I like to look to both Eastern and Western knowledge and philosophy. Then one finds a clear sense of both the physical and the metaphysical. As I said, I then work on openness. I would define the openness of the pharynx as the feeling of the smile (which raises the zygomatic arch and the soft palate), the feeling that one has before one yawns (which widens the pharynx), a released puckering forward of the lips (to help lengthen the vocal tract), and a releasing of the tongue root forward. I like to work with a fairly closed mouth in the mid range to help find the inner space. Many students seem to favor having an open mouth without actually opening the pharynx. I am looking for a long vocal tract. That requires a lowered larynx and a puckering forward of the lips. This longer vocal tract creates connectedness.

I don't address *range*. I don't try to stretch the instrument. I look first to develop a solid, connected, well-balanced middle and low range. I see that as the building block for the high voice. When the middle and lower registers function in a relaxed, well-oiled way, then I do a lot of work on the passaggio (the break between the middle and high registers). I believe in the two-pyramid theory of the passaggio. The passaggio is the place where the tips of both pyramids meet. I look for a very slender production there that I effect through closed vowels (specifically a closed /u/ or a closed /i/) that I use with closed, puckered lips. Then one lengthens the opening of the throat and mouth in an upward direction above the passaggio into the top. I attempt this only when the student has a functioning middle voice.

Resonance?

A balance of head and chest. I'm looking to get a release from the chest and make use of tracheal resonance, by openness and a release of the tongue, and a feeling of speaking from the level of the heart, speaking from the sternum. That is not pushing *into* the sternum; it is a release *from* it that comes from a very open throat, a released tongue, and a feeling that you are speaking in an intimate voice, rather than speaking to project. It's the way many film actors talk. They speak in a very intimate way because they know the boom mike is there. I'm looking for people to speak in that personal, connected way. From that connectedness, one then creates greater clarity of the speech, raises subglottal pressure, and the voice will begin to project, so it is then "intimate for thousands." That's what I am looking for in terms of sound: an intimate core that is then projected through the greater subglottal pressure of the person singing.

That's an interesting perspective and a visual that you've made extraordinarily clear. Now, articulation.

I work a lot on tongue tip and tongue root release, and I do that using the dental consonants without any "helping" movement of the jaw. With /l/, /t/, /d/, or /n/, I do exercises to get the tongue tip to raise and lower without the jaw helping. I also will work on the rest of the consonants with a thumb between the fingers. Not a cork, by the way, because with a cork you bite to hold it in place. I'm looking for the jaw to be completely relaxed and not bite, so I prefer people to use their thumb. If they bite their thumb, they'll know it by the pain (or at least the teeth marks) it creates. The singer learns to keep the jaw in a position of softness and rest, and articulate with a very agile tongue tip and lips. I'm looking for the lips to not pull back, because that shortens the vocal tract and raises the larynx. I work on articulation of all consonants for an agile tongue tip and released lips, tongue root, and jaw.

And finally, connection, or the acting dimension.

Well, I work on that a great deal. Certainly, there is no point in a person going out for an audition with that not being in place. I work from the approach of challenging and inspiring people's storytelling and specific acting choices, but I also simply help people by doing monologue work. First I'll take the text outside of the music and have the singer speak intimately from that connection on the sternum. The artist gets a sense of connection to breath and text with that. Then I challenge singers to be very specific and bold about their storytelling.

So you would have a student do a song or an aria as a spoken monologue first?

Generally, yes.

Again, from your perspective, how do these individual aspects of training relate to one another (1) in the learning process and (2) in performance?

Lamperti said something very important. He said that when you're a student, you employ objective learning and that is from the feet up. When you're a professional, you employ subjective learning and that is from the head down. I believe what he means by *objective learning* are the skills one needs, such as alignment, breathing, opening, clarity of speech, how to navigate the passaggio (the "break"), which you really do need to learn and practice with tremendous repetition in the way that dancers do their daily barre to automatize certain physical responses. However, when you perform, you perform from an artistic idea of the whole, how you're going to sound, how you're going to feel, the story you have to tell, the atmosphere you wish to create. So you're going to work with much more generalized principles that organize the many individual things that you have already automatized under one umbrella. You cannot be thinking about the individual pieces of your technique in a performance and expect to connect to your public.

Brilliant. Do you have any additional comments you'd like to make?

No. I really look forward to reading the book when it comes out.

PUBLICATIONS

Neil Semer, "Applying Chiaroscuro to Your Art and Life," *Classical Singer Magazine,* Volume 16, number 10. October 2003, 30.

———. "Musical Theatre Singing for the Classical Singer," *Classical Singer Magazine,* Volume 17, number 1. January 2004, 14.

———. "Are You a Plan A or Plan B Singer?" *Classical Singer Magazine,* Volume 17, number 8. August 2004, 41.

REFERENCE

Lamperti, G. B. 1931. *Vocal Wisdom.* Edited by W. E. Brown. Marlboro, NJ: Taplinger.

Web site: www.neilsemer.com

PART II

Interviews,
UNITED KINGDOM

7. MARY HAMMOND

Photography by John Clark

Mary Hammond has worked as a vocal coach and advisor with the first casts of more than twenty West End shows, including Les Miserables, Cats, Mamma Mia, *and* Rent, *and in 1993, she founded the musical theatre postgraduate course at the Royal Academy of Music in London. For over twenty-five years she worked as a singer in a wide range of styles and media, including opera at Covent Garden, stadium gigs with groups like Black Sabbath, Pink Floyd, and Roxy Music, as well as in television, radio, and film. In addition to being a vocal consultant to Cameron Mackintosh Ltd., the Really Useful Group, the Royal National Theatre, and other major production and touring companies, Mary serves as director and head of the musical theatre programme at the Royal Academy of Music. Her comments here provide an invaluable perspective on theatre in general and on the technical demands of singers in particular.*

Mary and I met in New York in January of 2001, during the second National Association of Teachers of Singing (NATS) Conference on Belting. Three years later, I gave her a call to discuss the focus of this book, and she graciously agreed to be interviewed at the Royal Academy of Music, between an afternoon workshop with Elton John and an evening meeting at the academy. Our discussion took place in a large, elegantly appointed conference room on a rainy afternoon in northwest London.

PERSPECTIVE

Will you say something about your background and about what influenced or informed your approach to teaching?

I trained in both singing and piano at the Royal Academy of Music. I worked mainly in the recording industry, live concerts (Royal Albert Hall, Barbican, Royal Festival Hall mainly), television, radio, and so on. The main working time was the late sixties through the early nineties, and the recording industry was quite prolific in London during that time. I worked for John McCarthy (the Ambrosian Singers) a lot, and the group recorded with all the prodigious conductors and singers of that time. We also did a lot of television and worked with a completely different style of singing. I seemed to be able to sing in different styles quite easily and didn't think about it. It was just a question of "getting the job done." It was necessary to listen, adapt, be quick. I suppose that this opportunity of listening to so many good performers/singers gave me a discerning ear without realizing it. When I began to teach—I think that I really *coached* at first—I was pleased to find the Association of Singing Teachers and, subsequently, the British Voice Association (BVA). Both these organizations have been a real lifeline for me.

How would you describe the vocal requirements for singers in musical theatre today? How have those requirements changed over the years and where do you think they're going?

Singers need to be extremely flexible in order to earn a living in musical theatre. No longer can you stay in one category. You need to be able to sing in many different styles and have a very adaptable voice.

What is your passion in this work?

I am passionate about the integration of acting and singing. I work a lot in live theatre and, therefore, am lucky enough to see the results of the hard work the students put in. I *love* theatre, and am always excited by it. It never grows stale, and my work doesn't become technique for its own sake, but serves a direct need. This suits my personality. My current phrase that I like is "Technique liberates your imagination."

*What role does voice science, or vocal anatomy and physiology, play
in your work with students or clients?*

I am totally indebted to my friends and colleagues in the BVA for learning about that aspect of this subject. I've learnt enough to know which
expert to ask for help if I need to. It's very comforting. I feel that teaching
singing carries with it a lot of responsibility and could be very lonely if you
couldn't share some of the problematic areas.

*Does movement or movement-based training play a role in your
teaching?*

My course at the Royal Academy of Music has daily physical warm-up and
movement, besides dance. I think physical strength is vitally important.
As the students get stronger, it has a *real* effect on their voices, in every
way. It has been nice to design a course that puts into place all the things
I believe in. I think *all* singing courses should include compulsory physical fitness classes. I think it would make a big difference.

Do you use any recording equipment in your studio?

I use a tape recorder and a microphone, if it is appropriate. I teach students
how to listen to themselves and what is useful about that. They can hear if
what they are thinking is coming through, articulation, and so on. Most
tape recorders aren't useful to listen for quality, but can be used for putting
down accompaniments and sometimes exercises. I sometimes video students; probably will do this more. It's most useful for them to realize that
if, for example, you are correcting posture, they can see what *you* can see.

THE TRAINING

*Where do you start? What are the foundational aspects of training
to which you regularly attend?*

I often ask someone to bring something they feel they can sing, and also
something they find difficult. This gives me some idea of what they are
thinking. Because I often teach professionals who have already trained, I
would ask them what they feel they need help with. Then I hear them sing
and make up my own mind. I like to feel that singers take responsibility for

their own voices. I don't like the "Svengali" approach where singers rely too much on their teachers. I think it's unhelpful and unhealthy. I look immediately for: (1) airflow; and (2) posture/spine, head and neck alignment. I always start with explaining quite physiologically how breath "works." I often ask students to explain to me what they understand. I think you have to make sure you speak the same language.

What do you expect to observe in a singer who is well trained or in a performer who sings well, with or without training?

A "free sound," a balanced body, and no unnecessary tensions.

Granted, the journey is different from one singer to another, but if you think it appropriate, would you cite a couple of examples of how students might get from A to B, or from their first lessons with you to a solid professional technique?

I think this is a huge subject! The answer briefly is: structured, diligent practice, a gradual building of "insularity"! I think you should always try to apply what you are teaching technically to a specific song the performer is studying. I'm very glad that I coach as well as teach technically, as I like to combine the two. In the search for a better ("perfect"!) voice, it is important to keep alive the love of singing and the joy of performing.

A "solid professional" technique takes a long time. I feel that most students in musical theatre have to consolidate their training while working. The average time in training is not really long enough.

In the answers to earlier questions, you have certainly touched on some, if not all, of the six aspects of training listed below:

Alignment, Breathing, Range, Resonance, Articulation, Connection (the Acting Dimension)

Now, from the perspective of your own approach, would you comment specifically on each of these technical elements, to whatever extent and in whatever order you choose?

Alignment. I think this is essential. I send performers to specialists—osteopaths or physiotherapists—if I feel there is a long-term problem that needs correcting. I think teachers need to learn as much possible about the balance of the body.

Breathing. I spend quite a while making sure the students/performers understand about abdominal release. I am also aware of quick clavicular breathing for pop or rock. I like the idea of "breath management" and air-flow. I don't use the word *support* too much; I think it's really important that students learn how easy it is to overbreathe and to "hold" the breath and have too much subglottic pressure. In some intense musical theatre, it is easy to let "passion" make you hold your breath, and to cause tension in an unhelpful way.

Range. This depends entirely on the type of song you are singing and how you choose to use your larynx. I try to keep a very flexible laryngeal involvement. Some students who have sung songs such as "Heaven on Their Mind" since they were at school, find those gymnastics really easy. I find that all the sounds that people who are now in their forties and fifties find difficult, the young performers find really easy. In the main, it's the "lower larynx" (in Jo Estill's language, *sob quality*) that young performers find less familiar. I never force range; it's often dictated by the musical they are in. I mostly teach professionals, so my job is to help them accomplish what they need to do. I feel they often have to sing a tessitura that is difficult for them. I think most musical theatre has extremes of range to match or express extremes of emotion.

Resonance. This varies enormously with the style. So much of musical theatre is a very "open sound," but I do teach a "forward" resonating sound as well.

Articulation. Just call me the "consonant queen"! I nag about this and do specific work on text constantly.

Connection. The link between acting and singing has fascinated me for a long time. I can't think about voice without thinking about relevance to the text. I spend a great deal of time linking music and language. I would expect a singing voice to be flexible enough to change in voice quality to express the text. Dynamics alone are not enough.

Again, from your perspective, how do these individual aspects of training relate to one another (1) in the learning process and (2) in performance?

The performance will be successful if the preparation has been meticulous. Again, imagination is served by technique.

Do you have additional comments you would like to make?

I think that there is so much contemporary music that uses a very light, rock sound, it is important to prepare the *whole* voice. I don't think we should get confused by *belting*, or *the mix*. All the terminology currently being used seems to be subjective. I think as long as the student and teacher agree on terminology, then that's okay.

I think what might slightly differ about my work is that I realize however much you may work technically in your studio, there are so many different things that happen when you perform. For example, alignment: Add to this dance and experience of emotions in acting terms. Air intake, ditto. How do you automatically release when your character is in an extreme of emotion? All of the technical work has to be directed and put into practice, ideally, when your student is developing a character. In musical theatre, you need to watch rehearsals and performances as much as possible and make useful comments.

A vocal coach's job is to listen to the director and the musical director and to try to facilitate the things they require if the performer is having difficulty. The worst thing is to interfere and put your own interpretation in the way. It's not your job in that instance.

8. Penni Harvey-Piper

It was a sunny day as I made my way to Wimbledon on the train. Crowds of people gathered outside the station; it was the height of the tennis season. Walk to the right up a long hill, then right again. Fewer people now and a lovely neighborhood. Humm. A gate—was this the house? I walked round to the right, rang the bell, and Penni answered, accompanied by the sweetest dog I've ever met. Then over tea and biscuits, we got acquainted and recorded the following interview.

Photography by Elliot Franks

I'd never met Penni Harvey-Piper but knew from her reputation that she was absolutely one of the top voice professionals in the UK. We'd spoken by phone and I'd sent her a copy of the interview questions. She was prepared with the photograph and other information I'd requested, and when I glanced at her CV, I was immediately struck by the last two items under Work Experience:

- singing teacher, with particular emphasis on natural and correct use of the body *and*
- occasional work as a secretary, barmaid, model, and petrol pump attendant.

I knew I was in for a treat!

PERSPECTIVE

In musical theatre one is mostly teaching actors, some of whom have never, ever sung before, and are terrified. I have a peculiar background in that I'm not a singer, so I understand how people feel about singing: "Oh, my god!" They're fine acting, but as soon as they have to sing, they turn to jelly. I did a degree at music college in piano and organ, did a lot of accompanying, but then I became an occupational therapist. I qualified in both the physical and the psychological, so I've done a lot of psychology and I've worked in mental homes and then finished up working for two or three years with cerebral palsy children, retraining the body patterns in normal and natural movement.

Oh, what a wonderful background this is!

Well, I think it's a perfect background for teaching musical theatre, because I honestly think a knowledge of psychology is number one in teaching nonsingers, teaching actors, and I think if you don't have that knowledge, or that expertise, you don't get on very quickly. I always tell pupils right from the start that I'm not a singer, and immediately that seems to relax them. My practice is mostly with actors, quite a few pop singers as well, but quite a lot of repair jobs.

Do you get regular referrals?

From laryngologists, and occasionally from opera singers, too, because I find that a lot of opera singers tend to lose their voices in their late forties, which, I believe, is because they've been taught the old-fashioned, "It's all in the diaphragm" way, and when you're supporting strongly from the diaphragm, you actually cannot stop tension in the neck, which is very interesting. After a while the vocal cords say, "Hang on, I've had enough," and as soon as I can get them to drop their support to where I think is the right place . . .

You mean, it's lower.

Really low. And as soon as I can do that, and once they accept it, their voices so far have always come back. Very interesting, this old-fashioned kind of thing still being taught, but I always start off by making people bark like a dog at their first lesson. If you make sound without thinking,

"Oh, I'm singing," and particularly if you think, "Oh, what a stupid thing to do," you just do it, then you feel what your body's doing, and that is how we are designed to produce sound. And if you work on the way we are designed to produce sound, you never get nodules.

I couldn't agree with you more!

I teach nonsingers to work in or even take leads in West End musicals. And usually, when I'm sent them by the management—they tend to pick actors they think would be great, and then, of course, send them off to have singing lessons. I usually get about eight weeks to teach them, which has a lot of influence on the way that I teach them, as opposed to somebody who's going to stay for a year or ten years or whatever. Eight weeks seems to be the limit Cameron Mackintosh allows, and Lloyd Webber, too. They think in eight weeks you can turn a nonsinger into a singer and take the lead in a West End musical! (Mind you, I usually manage to do it!)

So with those kind of eight-week people, I work from the acting first, how they would say something, feel that resonance, and feel that emotion. The only thing I always do on the first lesson is actually explain what the body is doing to produce sound, and in a very simplified way. I try to make them understand how the sound waves are made from the vocal cords, but sound waves are silent until they hit a surface, and when they do that dog, "woof, woof," or even "moo" like a cow, it's very forward. That's the ideal place because it's immediately below your antrums so you get that lovely resonance, so the low support and the forward sound are the two things that I try to make them really understand. And if they understand what they're doing, then that's half the confidence.

Penni, will you say a bit more about your background and about what influenced or informed your approach to teaching?

My father was a laryngologist. In fact, he was Winston Churchill's laryngologist and all during the war he was sitting beside him in the House of Commons with his throat spray. So, right from the beginning, I've been interested in voices. I got my music degree in piano and organ. Then when I had to stop work because I started having children, I went to work for another singing teacher who was a very good friend of ours, Ian Adam, who was the first teacher to specialize in musical theatre. I worked with him as his pianist for a few years and then he had a long waiting list and said, "Look, would I just start teaching 'so and so'?" because I knew as much about breathing as he did. So I took on two of his people on the waiting list, and by the end of the year I was working full time. I never meant to be a singing teacher. It came upon me. But I think it's the psychological and physical background that helps tremendously. Since then I've just become fascinated by the voice and passionate about it. Yes, I love my work.

Do you work with students on classical as well as musical theatre repertoire?

Yes, I do. I mean, not the eight-week ones, but all the other kinds of regular pupils. Oh, yes, most of my students study an aria or art song or something like that, and also learn differing styles. It's another thing I'm very keen on—understanding how to make different quality sounds, which to my mind is why opera singers cannot sing musical theatre. It drives me mad, because they all make such beautiful sounds. So I do a lot of making different sounds by lifting the tongue or various things, and teach them how to do rock and pop without getting nodules, and all with a forward resonance. If you keep the sound forward, you can make it sound like you're chesting; you can make it sound like you're doing a really heavy rock, but without any pressure on the throat. So I do teach lots of different textures and styles, particularly with musical theatre. Okay, so there is a specific style, but because it's theatre, they may have to sing something sounding as if they hate it. They hate that person, or they may have to sing something very gentle and sweet, and they've got to *know* how to change their voice to use it and explore it. Then it becomes so exciting to them and to me when they start exploring those sounds, and they suddenly realize they can do all sorts of things they'd never dreamed of.

How would you describe the vocal requirements for singers in musical theatre today? How have those requirements changed over the years and where do you think they're going?

I think the first thing is *stamina*, and knowledge, because if they know what they're doing, they have to be physically and mentally aware of what they can do, and basically, that's mostly down to the support. Secondly, they have got to realize that their body is their instrument, and if they break it they can't go and buy another string, so, again, I think it's terribly important that they get the strength and the knowledge. In old-fashioned musicals—I'm talking about prewar musicals—you had an introduction, you almost came out of the action and sang your song, and then went back into it. I think one of the great advantages nowadays—the thing that's changed—is the use of the microphone, so they don't always have to shout, but musicals are much more physical nowadays. It's much harder work. And a lot of the music is getting much more difficult to learn. A lot of the modern stuff is horrendous to learn.

Yes, both rhythmically and in terms of the pitch changes.

So they've got to be able to cope with it. They've got to do eight performances a week. Opera singers do two a week, and if they've got the slightest bit of sore throat, they cancel. These kids have got to go on eight times a week, so they've got to know what they're doing.

What is your passion in this work?

I'm passionate about passing on knowledge about what they're doing, and making them aware of how difficult it can be, but how easy they can make it. We all work too hard, particularly dancers. Their whole training is, if it doesn't hurt, they're not trying hard enough. So I always say to them, "If it hurts, you change your singing teacher, because you're doing something wrong." Also, a lot of people overmouth when they sing, so I get people occasionally to sing a couple of phrases with a pencil between their teeth, just so that they realize they can get a better forward sound that way.

What role does voice science, or vocal anatomy and physiology, play in your work?

First of all, I disagree a lot with making pupils focus on the larynx so that they lose that "What am I saying, why am I saying it, who am I saying it to?" Also, physiologically, you can talk about thickening the cords and doing all this sort of thing, but there are no voluntary nerve endings in the larynx, so it is not possible to physiologically control it. You know we've got two nervous systems?

Yes, the autonomic and the central.

There are no voluntary nerve endings from the back of the throat down, so we can't do anything consciously in the larynx. All right, you can do it by thinking sob or thinking scream, but you can't consciously, physically do it.

That's very interesting, Penni. Any other thoughts about anatomy and physiology?

I would say equally, *psychology*: anatomy, physiology, and psychology. I don't think they need to know the names of all the little muscles. I give them a diagram of the larynx and where the sound waves hit and I ask them to make a noise in their throat or make the noise from the back of the palate and then say, "Mama mia," and feel the different resonance. But they do need to know that all the vocal cords do is make the sound waves of the appropriate pitch.

Does movement or movement-based training play a role in your teaching?

Pilates a little bit, because Pilates is centered very low and they talk about *zip up*, and that's a perfect example for feeling that support.

Do you teach microphone techniques?

Yes, I do, particularly with regard to the way they hold their head. I make them work with my microphone and tell them to be absolutely adamant in the studio, if they're recording, that the microphone be in the right place. I usually say two things: "Treat the microphone as if it's your best friend's ear or as if you are talking to your best friend, and angle it from your mouth to the sixth row of the stalls," because that looks after the head position, unless, of course, you've got your director saying, "No, you must look up." So then I say, "Well, see if you can slightly move your body back but keep your chin in. Lift your head but keep your chin back."

THE TRAINING

*Where do you start? What are the foundational aspects of training
to which you regularly attend?*

I start by making them sing me a song—they all bring a song—so
I can just assess (a) that they can sing in tune and (b) whether they do
know what they're doing with their body and whether they're tense.
You look for all those things. From then on I just make them bark, then
I make them feel where the bark's coming from. Fascinating, when you
do bark, the jaw is perfect, and none of them realize that, so I've got a
mirror on the piano and I make them bark in front of the mirror to see
what the jaw's doing as they go up in pitch. Foundational aspects of
training? Basically, knowledge of your instrument, knowledge of how
the body works.

*What do you expect to observe in a singer who is well trained or in
a performer who sings well, with or without training?*

Ease and relaxation and no *visible* technique, unless it's put on for effect.
For instance, consciously taking a dramatic breath, just to add to the
dramatic effect. But I look for somebody who looks totally relaxed and
the sound just flows out like Ella Fitzgerald or Bing Crosby. They just
stand there and the sound comes out.

*In some American singers I'm noticing complete discombobulations
of the body on every inhalation, especially in belting, and a huge gasp
before every phrase.*

I haven't particularly noticed that happening over here. I teach a very
negative form of breathing. If they've pulled up for the support, at the
end of the phrase, actually all they have to do is think "Relax," and drop
the support.

There's a very nice image that one of my pupils told me of—he was
American actually and he'd been to New York University and done the
musical theatre course. He brought me back a lovely image of when you
want to take a deep breath you imagine you're filling your hip pockets.
That's very good if you've got a long phrase coming up, but the added

advantage of that also is that the breath is down there in your imagination, of course, so that your thoughts are still down there for that support.

Granted, the journey is different from one singer to another, but if you think it appropriate, would you cite a couple of examples of how students might get from A to B, or from their first lessons with you to a solid professional technique?

They must practice to get from a conscious technique to it becoming automatic. And the technique is relearning what your body would be doing if you had never had the lessons. But, to begin with, you have to do that technique consciously, and it only comes with constant practice, particularly when it's this eight-week thing. And they all do, they're very good. Most of them practice twice a day. You've got to form a habit, and that is really the way to get from A to B. You cannot rely upon having two or three lessons a week and let me do it for you. I'm not going to make their voice; they've got to do it themselves.

In the answers to earlier questions, you have touched on some, if not all, of the six aspects of training listed below:

Alignment, Breathing, Range, Resonance, Articulation, Connection (the Acting Dimension)

Now, from the perspective of your own approach, will you comment specifically on each of these technical elements, to whatever extent and in whatever order you choose?

Okay. *Alignment* is very important because that will center you. I say to my pupils, "Unless you are centered yourself, you cannot give," and performing is giving. If you are not totally aligned and at one with your body, you've got nowhere to give from, so alignment is very important.

For *breathing* I say, "Relax and allow nature to work, unless you have a big phrase coming up, and then you use your hip pockets."

Range. I think that's important, and, in fact, all my pupils, basically, have the same range, whether they're sopranos, altos, baritones, or tenors. The exercises stretch from the F below middle C to top C, and they all do that. So I think range is important, not necessarily because they might have to sing high, but because if they can sing high in the exercises, then something that's just an E on the top space is easy.

And the voice is richer.

Yes, I think it's important to work on the bottom of the voice as well, because I find that a lot of teachers just say, "You'll only need two or three of those notes; we'll work on the top." I've heard a lot of opera singers who've got fantastic top Cs, but nothing in the middle of the voice. They totally lose that focus. So, again, I tell them that it's just as important to work on the bottom because that wakes up lower overtones, which then come into the middle of the voice and make the whole voice much richer. You cannot just work on just one part of the voice. You've got to stretch it both ends.

Resonance. Absolutely vital for musical theatre, and as far as I'm concerned, your sound waves need to bounce around your top front teeth. I call it *musical theatre zing.* Without that, you can't communicate, because the resonance has got to be the same as where you would be speaking.

Articulation? Yes, important but it must be natural. It must be the way that people would be saying that phrase if they were just acting it, which again is what opera singers can't do. They have to enunciate every syllable. It's the weight on a syllable that matters.

Yes, the relative stress, rather than everything the same.

So it mustn't be overarticulated. I find that people tend to overarticulate like mad when they're first starting out, because they've watched *Top of the Pops* or something like that and everybody's overarticulating or overusing their mouths. I make them speak the phrase of the song first and see where they put the emphasis, and which little words they hardly do, and then just sing it like that, because then the phrase is interpreted and it's all about communication.

Connecting/the Acting Dimension. If you're connected emotionally, the technique will actually be there, because you cannot be emotional without that support. So the acting dimension is incredibly important. I find with natural singers, who've never had lessons, they're lovely to teach, because they have got a technique but they don't recognize it, and my job is not to change this, but to make them aware of what they are actually doing. They tend to fall down at auditions because they are so nervous that they can't use the emotion, so all you have to do is tell them what that emotion does in the body and relate to it. You've got to mean what you're saying, and even if you don't, if you hate the song and you've done it five hundred times already, if you are connecting through with your body, you *look* as if you're emotionally committed. So, very important.

Again, from your perspective, how do these individual aspects of training relate to one another (1) in the learning process and (2) in performance?

There's nothing worse than watching somebody in performance and thinking, "They're doing exactly what their singing teacher told them to do." I hate that. They're doing it all terribly correctly. This, I think, is where the practice comes in, because it should be a technique that becomes almost automatic. Once they start to perform, they should be able to forget about their technique with the confidence that it will be working, and maybe just pick out two or three points in the show where they've got to remember they must fill their hip pockets or they must remember to support for that top note or something like that. I think that's all one can hope for, so that they don't have to think technique all the time, but can concentrate on acting through the song.

Do you have additional comments you would like to make?

Yes, psychology, psychology, psychology. I think it's terribly important to make your student feel relaxed from the very first lesson. When you go to a first singing lesson, it's terrifying (I know—I've been there!). I think this house is great for teaching because it's a family house and we've got a very friendly dog. They all love the dog! The drawing room is a friendly room, but it's a family home, so we have grandchildren coming most weekends. It's a bit of a mess and that relaxes them, I think, to start, and we have an awful lot of laughter, which I think is very important. Laugh like mad. So that is important from the word *go*, to make them feel at home.

Also, *words*. Most of my exercises have got words in them, because, otherwise, the change from exercises just on vowel sounds to then singing a song appears to bear no relation. So nearly all my exercises have got words in them, and a lot of them I change every week, so that they don't get used to certain phrases. One or two exercises are just pure vowel sounds, but I should think about 60 percent of the exercises are on words, and I think that's important.

My summing up really is: It's the knowledge and the practice of how to change your quality, your style, and basically *know your voice*, know how it works. I think it's important that girls know things such as, before you start your menstrual cycle, the little glands that secrete lubrication on the cords dry up. It affects some people more than others, but with a lot of people they do find that once a month their voice changes and they don't know why and they don't relate it to a premenstrual phase. I think that kind of knowledge is so important. But also, things like, if you've split up with your partner, your voice is not going to work for you as well. All this is about the physical and the mental state and how it affects the voice, because you don't sing wonderfully unless you're really free. So they must know all those things so they don't get worried, "Why isn't the voice working?"

One other thing that I think is important is that students should leave their lesson feeling happy and fulfilled. We have a neighbor who told me that whenever she passes someone in our street who is skipping along and singing happily, she always knows they've just had a singing lesson. That, to me, says it all!

9. GILLYANNE KAYES

I met Gillyanne Kayes in 1998, when she was in the forefront of EVTS (Estill) training in the UK and Europe. As a course participant in Liverpool, I recall being thoroughly impressed by the gracious manner in which she related to one-hundred-plus lively voice teachers from around the world. Then when her first book, Singing and the Actor, *appeared in 2000, I became aware of her passion for voice as a single instrument.*

Photography by Jeremy Fisher

Gillyanne Kayes is cofounder of the multidisciplinary voice training company Vocal Process, and creator of Integrated Voice, the pedagogy program offering cross-genre training to teachers of singing and theatre voice. As a freelance writer, teacher, and voice specialist, she travels widely giving presentations, seminars, and master classes. The following interview was recorded at her home studio in southeast London, on a gloriously bright summer afternoon.

PERSPECTIVE

Where and whom do you teach? Who are your students or clients?

I'm pretty well freelance now because of running my own voice training company. We have a huge range of clients, so in a workshop or training situation I might be working with a total beginner who wants to sing pop, or a classical singer who is curious about crossover. There again I might be working with a voice and speech teacher, or speech and language therapist who wants to know more about the physicality of producing voice in order to help their own clients. In my private studio, I work mostly with actors and musical theatre singers. I also mentor other singing teachers; they'll come to have a lesson and sort-of-brainstorming session with me. The mentoring is something that has grown over the last few years, because I have a huge interest in teaching teachers. Institution-wise, I work on a freelance basis on the MA [Master of Arts] voice course at Central, where I give a pedagogy unit in their final term. The focus is on diagnostic, using the work that we teach in our company, some of which has a base in the Estill vocal figure work. So exploring topics such as accessing different vocal qualities, defining the vocal setup that creates a particular sound quality, and developing auditory skills for good diagnostic. I really enjoy working with voice and speech teachers. I hadn't trained in text, but it's fun to work on the voice production side and see how the things that I've been using for a long time with singers work also in spoken voice. During this last year I've also started teaching on the MA musical theatre performance course at the Royal Scottish Academy of Music and Drama [RSAMD], where I act as the course vocal consultant.

How exciting!

This is a new MA course, created by Dr. Donna Soto-Morettini. I devised all the singing units for the course. They've just done their first showcase and there's a cohort of only twelve students, which is great. Another regular teaching trip is in Barcelona at ESMUC, the Escola Superior de Musica de Catalunya. It's not like our conservatoires here, more like a university setup where they offer jazz, Catalán folk music, early music, contemporary music, and so on. It is multi-genre, rather like my own client base. I'll go to teach there for three or four days at a time.

Do you speak Spanish?

I don't, no. I can speak a little, but they prefer to speak Catalán there anyway. So I have a translator, someone who's taken several training courses with me and is very good.

Would you say something about your background and about what influenced or informed your approach to teaching?

I trained as a classical musician and singer. I have a BA in music from the University of York. Initially, I was interested in early music and then later in Lieder. In fact, I worked with one of the great Lieder singers, Ilse Wolf, and she really engendered in me that interest in words linked with song. I wasn't very interested, at that stage, in opera, but it was the excitement of the words, I think, that helped me enormously when I began working with actors. So I worked as a classical singer for over ten years, though in some ways not very successfully. I did not have a good technique. I didn't really know what I was doing, and that didn't make me very happy as a performer. There are some performers who really aren't interested in what's happening mechanically, so long as they can do it. I wasn't like that; I was very unsure and, to be honest, looking back, I'm not a performing mentality. I don't have the killer instinct in *that* environment. So what happened then? Like most performers, I was doing a bit of teaching on the side: piano, singing.

So did you start out as a pianist?

No, I always wanted to sing, but I'd been advised to learn piano—and thank god! I would not have had the career I've had if I couldn't play piano. I don't play fantastically, but I do play. So I was teaching from home and in a girls' school, and then one of the big change points was my being asked to go and teach at the East 15 Acting School.

Did you know Andrew Wade there?

I did. Andrew and I did a lot of work together. When I was interviewed for the job, they asked me if I would be prepared to work with small groups of students and I thought, "Yes, I think I could handle groups." My first class was twenty students. I'd had no training as a teacher, none whatsoever! It was a very interesting experience because, very fast, I had to make the decision that all of them *could* do it, if only they knew how. And what the experience of East 15 taught me was that if you're looking at classical singing pedagogy (which is mostly what's been written about, researched, and is "known"), I think that most people who go for singing lessons can already sing. So when you start working with someone who can't pitch or who has, as I later found out, so much constriction that they're making a raspy sound, or they've got a range of about five notes, what are you going to do with them? Nothing in my experience as a singer had prepared me for that. Mum always sang, I sang at home, we could all sing, so I can't remember not singing in tune. So I set about finding out *how* to sing, mostly by applying the bodywork I was learning, which I would say is closest to Feldenkrais. And what I noticed was that Andrew had a *methodology*. I'd not come across this. Singing teachers had ideas; they had prejudices. But here was someone with a methodology. I was fascinated by that, so the path that I went on for the next few years, until I came across Jo Estill and her work, was really based on British voice training, body alignment, vowel placement, and a physical awareness of what you were doing. Andrew and I collaborated a lot and before he got really busy at the RSC, we did quite a number of workshops together. Andrew would do the text work and I would do the singing. He was so open and wonderful to work with. And then I worked at Rose Bruford College, and Lyn Darnley was there.

Oh, yes. I did one of my teaching practices at Rose Bruford and worked with Lyn.

That was another very happy collaboration. Interestingly, as a freelance at Rose Bruford, I had a horrible timetable. I worked two days back to back, eight hours of solid teaching with an hour for lunch. Four classes of an hour each with a nominal five minutes in between (if the students would let you have it), followed by four hours of one to one in fifteen-minute units. Of course, I started losing my voice and ended up in a voice clinic. When they examined me, I sang a few notes, and they said, "Well, it's not your singing; it's your speaking." They sent me to speech therapy, which, I have to say, was completely useless. It was all about hydration, hydration, hydration, which was fine as far as it goes, and then, basically, very, very soft voicing. And I said, "Look, I'm working with a group of fifteen actors. This is not going to help." So I went to Lyn and said, "Look, you must know these secrets." And so we did some work together—skill swapped—and she helped me with my glottal attacks. I wasn't using my airflow in speech, I'd got my family speech patterns, and I just wasn't really applying . . .

. . . what you **knew** *as a singer.*

You see, what I'd always been told as a singer was, as a soprano, I was supposed to speak in my head voice [demonstrating] and then I wouldn't damage my voice.

Yes, there are lots of people who still believe that.

Well, it's actually not a healthy mode of spoken delivery, so Lyn was able to help me with that. At that time I also had private clients, and then I joined the British Voice Association. I'd always been interested in physiology and anatomy. I would love, at school, to have done anatomy, but it wasn't on the curriculum. And then Jo Estill came to town and the first thing of hers that I went to was a workshop comparing opera with belting. Well, it was all quite shocking, all those glottal onsets when I'd been learning how to avoid them and making sure to connect with the breath! Then when a course of Jo Estill's was set up, I hummed and hawed about going on it because I thought, "I don't know if I want to learn this because she doesn't talk about the body; she doesn't talk about breath." But Janice Chapman, a colleague at the British Voice Association and a very fine operatic teacher, persuaded me to go on the course. She said, "If you learn one thing, learn about retraction and it's worth your money." So I thought, "Okay, I'll go." So I went and, as you can imagine, it was all quite a baptism of fire. There was plenty of on-course uproar. Jo is very contentious in the way that she teaches.

Yes, I know.

Nevertheless, I went away after the five days and started trying things out. I remember that one key thing for me was, "Raise the back of the tongue for high notes." I'd been doing so much bodywork, relaxing and letting go, that I thought this idea was nonsense. But when I went home and looked in the mirror (because I was preparing a concert at that time), sure enough, I could see the back of my tongue coming up when I went up to a top A. And, of course, I'd been telling my students to do the opposite! So I went back to the college where I was working, and to one particular girl who'd had a very poor range, I said, "I'll tell you what. We'll do something different today. We'll raise the tongue." Out came the top notes, and I began to realize that there was something very practical about Estill's work that made sense to me. And I started using the work almost straightaway (I'm like that), using the two or three things I thought I could handle and that were good. I did this with my students at Rose Bruford and I absolutely leveled with them. "I've been on this course. I think some of this work's good. We're going to do it." Well, of course, they'd spent most of a year lying on the floor, improvising, singing notes feeling good, humming, and relaxing, and here I was getting them to "feel things" in their larynx. They hated it! They absolutely loathed it. But after about three weeks they began to build an internal feedback that they could relate to, and I noticed that the two worst singers in the group—girls who were vocally raspy and constricted—suddenly improved dramatically. I went on from there with the application of the parts of the Estill work that I felt I could handle. It took me a while. I always used it in conjunction with breath work and what I knew of bodywork, but now there was less class time spent on the bodywork and more on the vocal tract. I also found that, as a result, I needed to spend less time on breathing because things were starting to function in the vocal tract more efficiently. Now, around the same time, I also did some work with Janice Chapman. I realized that I'd always been confused by the information given about breathing technique in singing. I'd been taught to lift your ribs and hold.

Rib reserve.

Yes, rib reserve. And then, of course, the "release" thing was becoming more important, in spoken voice work. So there was a conflict. I knew things were going on in my abdominal wall, but as a singer had also been told that you weren't supposed to feel anything there. So I asked Janice, "You know about this abdominal wall stuff, don't you? What's actually going on here?" And she taught me her work on the "diamond" and the abdominal release work that's based on the Accent Method. It was heaven to this low-grade asthmatic. Personally, I found it enormously helpful and, after that, I stopped doing rib work, frankly, because, as far as I'm concerned, if you're already fighting gravity, why add to the load? And it also tied in with the Feldenkrais-type bodywork I had been using in my teaching.

What I then became fascinated by, with regard to the Estill work, was the physiology and anatomy of the vocal function. And that was how I got together with Meribeth Bunch.

She's been one of my mentors as well.

When I first met Meribeth, I was organizing courses for Jo Estill in the UK. We had about a hundred people on a range of courses. At that time I wasn't a licensed Estill trainer, so I wasn't teaching on the course and Meribeth and I sat together on the front row. I quickly realized that she would probably be able to fill in the physiology and anatomy gaps that I had begun to realize were there in the understanding of Estill's work. So I asked her if she would start teaching a vocal anatomy course for those of us who'd done Estill and wanted to go deeper. And so it was great to have that information about vocal function at last and I knew that I'd got the tools to go away and look things up and work them out for myself. So it's been a brilliant journey, and I'm very happy to be in the place that I've grown to now, which is—you've got a question further down saying, "What drives me?"

Yes, just skip to that. We'll go back to the others.

What drives me is enabling people's voices to work. What drives me is *what* makes the voice work. I find everything about voices totally fascinating and I shall probably continue along that path until I'm ready to stop. I suppose in that sense, I am mostly known for being a technician, and I make no apology for it . . .

Why should you?

. . . because technicians are needed. I think that most problems with the voice are, frankly, functional, and I get very irritated with practitioners and teachers who say, "Oh, it's in your head." I say, "No, it's not in your head. It's in your muscles." That said, of course, there are sometimes psychological blocks that people do have to work through.

How would you describe the vocal requirements for singers in musical theatre today? How have those requirements changed over the years and where do you think they're going?

Okay, I'll answer the second half of the question first. Certainly in the UK, I think *Les Mis* was a watershed. Until that time, you would always have certain roles in a musical where the actor was required to maybe belt or sing in what I would define as a speech-like quality, or a twangy quality, usually a character part. But on the whole, singing was more lyrical and had closer links with a classical setup, closer to operetta. When *Les Mis* came on the scene, people were suddenly being asked to find a different kind of sound quality, something more dramatic and realistic, what we've called in *Successful Singing Auditions* a musical theatre *verismo* style. Something darker, more gritty, more gutsy. And at the same time—I'm thinking of Andrew Lloyd Webber's writing—also coming into vogue was more of a "pop" or commercial sound. So these other vocal styles started to creep into theatre and I think have greatly influenced its current development. Frankly, what was happening at the time was that we teachers were running around trying to help people to find these sounds. Teaching in drama school, this was interesting. All the kids were bringing in this new stuff, the *Starlight Express* and the *Les Mis* stuff, and I'd be training them to sing mostly in their head voice (because that was the training I'd had) and maybe just a little bit of chest voice occasionally. And their response would be, "But in *Les Mis* they're singing like *this*, and I'm not going to get work singing like that." And that was actually what took me to the Estill work initially. I had a student who could belt and I didn't know what she was doing. I taught her to sing "properly" and she could still belt. So I do think that around that time there was a big shift in what actors were expected to do. Directors were not accepting the "voice beautiful" any more; they were looking, at best, for a real union between the dramatic content and the vocal quality; at worst, they or the producers were looking for something more commercial. I think both of those elements have continued side by side and they're certainly influencing musical theatre today because now we have musicals like *Tonight's the Night*, where the young man doing the lead is trying to imitate that very raspy Rod Stewart sound. So people are also being asked to mimic voices and vocal qualities of other artists. We also now have immensely long-running shows. I think we've lost some of that creativity of being able to invent and vocally characterize and, sadly, that is what is going on in musical theatre at the moment.

What role does voice science, or vocal anatomy and physiology, play in your work with students or clients?

It's quite big, but I think what's important is to know when to invoke it. Some clients really don't need a lot of that type of information. What's important, I think, is for the teacher to know the information, to have that background, and to be able to use it in a way that enables students or clients to process the information in a way that is appropriate for them.

Does movement or movement-based training play a role in your teaching?

I'd say that my work is informed by my experience of the Feldenkrais work. I also still do yoga, as you know, and I will certainly physically adjust people, if required, during a lesson or workshop, but I don't feel that I'm particularly expert in that area.

The Training

Where do you start? What are the vital signs you check right away when a student comes to you? What are the foundational aspects of training to which you regularly attend?

The first thing I ask is "How efficient is their habitual voice use?" Things to look out for might be whether their habitual voice is breathy or creaky, or if they seem to have a posterior glottal chink, if they speak with constriction. What's their speaking range? Is there much resonance there? When they started to sing, I would be listening for their habitual mode in singing, because often people will have a mode that they like best. How do they onset with the breath? Is it always in a particular way? What kind of ability do they have to manage the range? This is always a big one for me. Are there signs of constriction? Is the tone clear? Posture, breath use, habitual setup, ability to maneuver the vocal tract. What about the tongue, lips? Is their production habitually nasal? And then discussing with them—I think this is *very* important—finding out what language the student uses. What are their concepts? Do they think they're singing on a column of air and the voice is sort of bouncing on top of it? Do they talk about head and chest voice, and what are the terminologies that are meaningful to them? I think, as I've become more experienced as a teacher over the last twenty-five years, you can instruct students, but if they don't cancel the previous order—it's like a computer that's already got a route in there—if you don't find out what that route is and cancel it, they may not be able to accept new instructions. And it doesn't matter how hard they try because the original instruction takes priority. And so I will discuss the language they're using, and occasionally I will suggest that they might like to explore a different way of thinking about something. From a client point of view, I would normally discuss an agenda with them in the early stages of training. What is appropriate for them? What are they looking for? Setting an agenda makes it easier for them to achieve their aims.

What do you expect to observe in a singer who is well trained or in a performer who sings well, with or without training?

Ability to grade dynamically. That's very important, not always at one level. Ease through the range, ability to communicate text through song if we're looking at musical theatre. Pop songs often aren't text-based: They're voice-based; they're emotion/feel-based. Ability to handle style, and I suppose that other thing which I call the X factor, which is vocal/physical presence. Somebody can have that and, frankly, maybe not sing technically very well.

But that can override.

Yes.

Granted, the journey is different from one singer to another, but if you think it appropriate, would you cite a couple of examples of how students might get from A to B, or from their first lessons with you to a solid professional technique?

Okay, I can give you two different examples that might be interesting. One guy came to me who is a recorded jazz artist. He has a good reputation in the UK and is expanding into the international market. He came to me because he felt that his voice was in trouble and he was getting quite a lot of gigs and so wanted to make sure he was healthy. He felt he was having difficulty negotiating a certain part of his range and he wanted help with that. So I listened to some of his recordings; I listened to the way that he was singing and to the way that he was speaking. He comes from the south of Ireland and has a very soft-spoken quality. So that's his habitual speaking pattern and, of course, that kind of sound quality, which I define as a light, breathy speech, is used quite a lot in jazz singing. Jazz singing is mostly subtle. Coincidentally, he'd also joined a gospel choir because he was aware that he needed to develop a bit more balls in his sound and he was belting away up there at the top of his range, and somehow he'd got caught between these two things he was doing. My work with him was on getting him to realize how his particular instrument works. I could tell by his range that he had a bass instrument. He had a big larynx, long tube, wide tube. With permission from students, I do sometimes feel! And so I started to work with him to say, "Where is that gear change? (He talked about chest, falsetto.) How are you going to negotiate it?" And what he was tending to do was to try and force a powered falsetto sound into the upper range, and he couldn't get a clear tone. So initially we worked on getting his everyday chest voice/modal voice/speech quality working properly. And then finding out from that where the passaggio is, finding the options for moving through that passaggio so that you can get a clear tone with more volume if you want, how to manage falsetto if you're going to go there, and so on. And he was very, very pleased. We had about six or seven classes altogether and he felt he was much healthier afterwards. That was a very specific journey sorting out a particular difficulty.

Now another person would be—this is another guy. Is that all right? Do you mind?

No, that's fine.

Okay, this is a young man who came to RSAMD. I think he'd done quite a lot of amateur singing beforehand and had trained in a particular approach since before puberty. Physically he is tall and thin and though he's about twenty now, he's in that young man stage where he just hasn't filled out: He's floppy, he's all over the place. Great instinctive musicality and grasp of style. When he first started singing for me, he produced this strange sort of breathy voice and, when I spoke to him about his idea of voicing, the imagery was, "You float everything here" (with gestures around the top of the head and the forehead). So I said, "That's great. You're doing that extremely well." But there was no volume, there was no meat in the sound because the vocal folds simply were not used to coming together. He was very good doing pop repertoire, singing with a kind of a light voice that worked well with a microphone. And what I discovered was that, as I suspected, he'd sung with the same technical approach right through adolescence. So he was still singing with some of the sensations and setup of preadolescence, and this is something I find quite a lot in tertiary education, in undergraduates, young men. They haven't totally found their adult male voice. So we did a lot of airflow work and then connecting with the glottal onset, so that we could get a sense of the vocal folds being resistant to the breath. Voiced fricatives were very good from that point of view, for making sure that the airflow was sufficient, and suddenly we started to get a lot more ballsy sound out of him. He was singing as a high tenor then. This boy has a fantastic ear and an excellent instinct for musical style. He still has to watch things like his airflow, because he's such a committed actor that he forgets to just *allow* the emotional flow and to let the abdominal breathing really work for him so he doesn't start gripping vocally. He takes his passion into the vocal folds and an actor must learn how to commit to the text vocally without causing damage. I was actually quite worried the first time I heard him sing because I thought, "Why has he been let on this course? I don't think this boy can sing." And he made a huge journey in a year. There's a follow-up to the story, which is that this young man, nearly a year out of college, has physically filled out and his voice has dropped further. A late developer, he is now reworking his voice with me as a high baritone.

That's very exciting.

It has been a fascinating journey. So I look and listen for patterns that might need to be changed, and I talk a lot to my students about the passaggio and the ways of negotiating it—there isn't just one way—so that they get to know where it is and that it's not some kind of big deal that has to be avoided. I also teach them how to find the setups for different voice qualities at points in their training where I think it's appropriate.

In the answers to earlier questions, you have touched on some, if not all, of the six aspects of training listed below:

Alignment, Breathing, Range, Resonance, Articulation, Connection (the Acting Dimension)

Now, from the perspective of your own approach, would you comment specifically on each of these technical elements, to whatever extent and in whatever order you choose?

You know, I wanted to add: *phonation, phonation, phonation!*

Of course, from your perspective. The items I've listed tend to figure prominently in theatre voice training.

Yes, I know. These are the big ones. If you wanted to put it in a theatre context, I would say *breath* and *voicing*, and I would work that way so that, starting with *breathing*, I would be looking at receiving the breath, which is, to me, the most important thing. Exploring the relationship between breath and voicing, and different levels of resistance, flexibility. My approach is with abdominal breathing. That's the work that I do.

Yes, I love your section on breathing in Singing *and the* Actor.

Thank you. So all aspects of abdominal breath work would be in there, but very much in relation to phonation.

In terms of *alignment*, for me, it's very important for vocalists to know how they relate to gravity, how they are able to balance. The postural alignment has got to be such that it gives access to the abdominal breathing, and, for me, that means working some of the muscles of the back so that the front can be free. And because the voice is a suspensory mechanism, I talk to people a lot about the need for having the casing available so that it's stabilized: the importance of the head and neck balance outside to stabilize the mechanism inside, and also to assist in stabilizing against the breath when you're doing big voicing. I would include in alignment, bodywork that I've called *anchoring*, or the voice-body connection, which I believe is so important in big voicing.

Range?

Yes, I do *range* work. It's essential. In singing it's so rare to find a song that goes through less than ten notes, and, sure enough, if you've got ten notes to sing, you're going to have to negotiate the passaggio, so a lot of my work is negotiating the first passaggio and then, later on, the second, charting your range. It's a bit of a truism in *Singing and the Actor*, that people end up with a two and a half–to three-octave range, but actually they do, in terms of what their voice can achieve mechanically. I'd say as well in terms of range (and this is a more recent development in my approach), getting people to find what's their comfort zone, that it's okay to work in your comfort zone because that has a relationship to what is your voice type.

I find that voice types are not always recognized in musical theatre. In classical music, there's this whole *Fach* thing and we need it in musical theatre as well. For instance, there are soprano belters and there are mezzo belters, and they don't belt in the same part of the range, or they certainly don't belt the same range of notes. And the sound quality is different. A dramatic voice in musical theatre has to be handled differently from a more lyric instrument. Can the lyric instrument perform dramatically? Yes it can, but it has to be handled differently. So I'd put these issues under range and possibly under resonance as well.

Resonance. It's such a big subject. Balance of nasal/oral resonance, the resonance that comes from opening inside the larynx at the level of the vocal folds—that area is very important. Between the back of the tongue and the pharyngeal wall is also a very important area for me, so that you don't get that area cramped. I also work on twang with my singers for brightness and projecting power, and I work on developing forward resonance, using the muscles of the face, using the mask. Chest resonance is not a term I use much except to cross-refer; I tend to go there by talking about what the vocal folds are doing, so I might talk about the chest mechanism, which I identify as *speech quality*.

Now to *articulation*: With singers you've got two areas. You've got articulation of notes, which could include how you move your voice between pitches and that whole flexibility thing, which with some singers needs attention. And then you've got articulation of consonants and placement of vowels: an enormously important subject. The management of vowel placement in singing, I think, is sometimes a misunderstood subject because what's often happening is that in order to create a certain kind of resonance, the vowel placement is fixed in a particular way, and that certainly has a knock-on [secondary] effect in theatre singing because it can lead to not singing the vowels that are in the text and in the world of the song. So you get all kinds of distortion, all kinds of compromises made. While I'm not a specialist in accents, I will encourage and help my students to work within the speech patterns and accent of the character that they are preparing.

So that when they start to sing, they aren't suddenly a different person.

Absolutely. It's got to be believable as the same person. And also the whole business of how you articulate the consonants when you are dealing with pitch, because the pitching mechanism and its needs can interfere with consonant articulation. So things that an actor would never do in spoken text, like scooping on a voiced fricative, will suddenly appear when they're singing because the whole consonant thing needs to be managed slightly differently in singing. I teach that consonants interrupt the vocal line—that they stop it—because that's what they do. And again, how to manage that and then how to give the *impression* of the vocal line when it's required, by using commitment. It's the commitment that carries the line and not the "smooth, uninterrupted flow" of breath, which is what we were all taught when we were training as classical singers.

I would say that *connection* comes mostly from the text: really exploring the text, finding those nuances within the text, working out the journey that you're going through in the song. The function of the song, what is the song actually doing at that point in the musical? Or if you're doing a song in cabaret, then obviously the function is different. You're going to be crossing the fourth wall and so on. If you're doing a pop song, you might want to convey some kind of feel or you want to make a particular sound. So when you're working with a classical singer (this is a bit of a generalization), the sense of emotional connection is in broad, grand sweeps—it's more generalized. Whereas when you're working with musical theatre text, it's more specific and detailed. There need to be more changes, and more dramatic changes. When I'm teaching *connection*, I use musicianship—for example, different ways of working a phrase, where the peaks are in the phrase—and I know that actors who can't read a note find this approach enormously helpful. And then finally, in terms of connection, looking at how you *play* the song in the physical space, who's in that space with you, and so on.

Again, from your perspective, how do these individual aspects of training relate to one another (1) in the learning process and (2) in performance?

One to five serve six, and in a sense, they need to appear as though they're instinctive and not planned. Occasionally, one has to have a monitor on, but the audience need not be aware of that monitoring. In terms of the learning process, sometimes it's quite difficult to get a student to see the point of doing a particular exercise. For example, the average actor simply does not want to do Ah—[demonstrates a vocalise]. Why? Why am I doing this?

When am I going to sing "Ah" on stage? And I suppose one of the things that I liked about the Estill work was that it's not vocalise-based, so it's quite easy to go quickly into applying it into song. I try very early on to bring song material into the equation, even if it's a question of something that the student already knows or we can rework together. With pop singers, if you can't show them pretty quickly how the work applies, they don't come back. So I think as a teacher you always have to be creative, even when you're working on something that is apparently quite technical. They need to see how it's going to relate to the impulse; otherwise, they're not going to be motivated to do it.

Do you have any additional comments you'd like to make?

I don't think I do, no.

PUBLICATIONS

Kayes, G. 2004. *Singing and the Actor*, 2nd ed. London: A & C Black (UK); New York: Routledge (USA and Canada).

———. 2004. *Singing and the Actor Audio Guide*. London: Gillyanne Kayes.

Kayes, G., & Fisher, J. 2002. *Successful Singing Auditions*. London: A & C Black (UK); New York: Routledge (USA and Canada).

Kayes, G. 2007. *Voicebox Videos: Looking at a Voice, Modal to Falsetto, Constriction and Release*. Endoscopy ebook: London: Gillyanne Kayes.

Web site: www.vocalprocess.co.uk

PART III

Interviews, Australia

10. LISA RYAN-MCLAUGHLIN

As I began to explore the musical theatre scene in Australia, I discovered rather quickly that it was spread out, rather than concentrated in a Broadway or a West End. So I went first to Brisbane, which was Photography by Jose McLaughlin *like coming "home" to a city I'd fallen in love with in the fall of 2000 during the Fifth Voice Symposium of Australia.*

It was early afternoon when Lisa Ryan-McLaughlin came in by train from the Gold Coast to meet me at my hotel. We'd communicated via e-mail but had never met. What a pleasure, and what a delightful couple of hours we spent taping discussions that rambled far afield of the interview questions.

Lisa Ryan-McLaughlin began her performing career as a teenager in Melbourne, singing on national television, doing cabaret, and touring internationally with a vocal trio. Her solo career has spanned over forty years and includes a full range of contemporary voice work, from jazz to rock to rhythm and blues and musical theatre. She is on the faculty of Queensland Conservatorium, Griffith University; maintains a private studio; and has worked extensively as a vocal coach in the corporate sector.

PERSPECTIVE

Will you say something about your background and about what influenced or informed your approach to teaching?

My background is as a performer, of course. I started off in television in Victoria. In the 1960s, variety, cabaret was very big and there was so much television. I didn't do much live entertaining, maybe a little performing in cafés when I was at school. Being a contemporary musician, there was nothing on offer in the way of education, so I was initially trained by an opera singer and classical teacher. Then I changed when I was about fourteen and went to a contemporary teacher who was associated with a television studio. I started out with a three-piece vocal group, doing very modern arrangements, and then moved from that into theatre. Moved up to Queensland when I was about thirty. I toured overseas for about five years, mostly Asia because of the Vietnam War, and there was a lot of work. I did that up to the mid-seventies. As a performer I met a lot of young singers and they'd say, "Would you teach me?" So then, as these things do, it snowballed and I had a large private studio of thirty to forty students. I also branched out more into television production and live production of shows and concerts. Then we formed an association on the Gold Coast of professional musicians and from that devised an awards program for young musicians that became a huge annual event. We used to call it Gold Coast Oscars, or Emmys, or Grammys. And I was still doing shows myself, was flying down to Sydney and Melbourne.

Then I was approached by a university in Lismore, which is in northern New South Wales, called Southern Cross University. At that stage it was called University of New England, Northern Rivers, and the bass lecturer, with whom I'd worked, rang me and said, "Would you be interested in coming in and talking to us about teaching at university?" And I said, "Well, I don't have a university degree." And he said, "No, we'd like you to come and talk to us." So I went down and met with the dean of music and they said, "We'd like you to come and work for us," and I thought it was just hysterical. However, that started me on this whole other career of university teaching and I now have a master of music degree and a graduate certificate of higher education. So I was there for four years before Warner Village theme parks approached me and I worked almost full time for them for about five years.

Then I was asked to apply to the Conservatorium. They asked if I would take on the jazz vocal ensemble, the choral ensemble, which I love, and then the director came to me and said, "You have a bit of a background in musical theatre." And I said, "Yes, not huge," but I was also an acting teacher. "Would you take over the class?" [he asked.] "Well, okay, I'll try it for a semester." That was six years ago. So it's really good. It's always a small class of about twelve to fifteen students, and the students come from across the Conservatoire, the consort.

Is there a musical theatre degree?

No, it's what we call a course, which is a subject.

You mentioned that you teach acting. Where did that come in?

Because of my interest in musical theatre, I obviously studied in Melbourne and had a marvelous teacher who, as life does these things to you, is now my colleague at Warner Village.

You said, "Obviously I went to Melbourne." So is Melbourne the hub?

It's really the center, although if you talk to a Sydney actor, Sydney's where it's happening. I still think Melbourne is where it's at, in terms of establishing yourself in a career in theatre. Melbourne has bigger cultural diversity, quite a lot more fringe theatre, and there are some marvelous acting teachers there.

How would you describe the vocal requirements for singers in musical theatre today? How have those requirements changed over the years and where do you think they're going?

I think you have to be able to cross the genres, probably leaning more to the contemporary than to the classically trained voice. However, I still feel that with classical voice training, singers have much stronger physicality. We are definitely, in contemporary, becoming much more aware of the pedagogical aspects of voice teaching. All our students, for instance, who are contemporary voice programme, have to sit technical exams on physiology. They have to understand. But we don't tend to engage the same amount of muscles, especially from the laryngeal muscles down, as does an opera singer. And I notice a difference in the quality of the voices; the classical voices are much bigger than our contemporary voices, but our contemporary voices can emote better. So I try and get a balance going, to give the classical singers more of an idea of speech quality and of using the vibrato more as an effect than as a necessity for every note. And I try to get the contemporary singers much more into their breathing, more into developing the musculature for the support mechanisms, for the bracing and anchoring of the body. I'm not a great believer in heavy belt; I teach a mix of thick and thin folds and speech quality, which is what I've always used. There's a lot of argument, even in the contemporary field. I have colleagues who believe every female can belt up to B flats in true thick folds. Okay, maybe they can eventually, but do they need to? Because they can produce as good a musical theatre sound with a mix, and it will last them forever.

And as teachers we really have to look after that.

We do.

Any thoughts about the direction that musical theatre is going?

Yes. Since the 1940s anyway, musical theatre has been the voice of society. If you go back even as far as *Guys and Dolls*, that was a statement about society. *South Pacific*, a statement about racism, and it's still relevant, but then you look at *Rent* and the contemporary musicals. They've got to take on the musical styles that the young people are listening to or they're going to be absolutely irrelevant. Of course, there will always be the revivals, which are wonderful.

And so the musical theatre singer has to do those, too.

Absolutely, and they have to be able to take on the modern influences. They've got to be melismatic, if necessary, to get the contemporary styling, but they've also got to be able to sustain an Adelaide from *Guys and Dolls*. So if they want any kind of a career, they've got to cross the genres.

Why do you teach what you teach? What is your passion in this work?

It's funny, isn't it? Teaching becomes part of your lifeblood.

Oh, yes.

I'm passionate about music. I live in a very musical house; my husband is a brilliant musician. Our lives are music. Then, of course, developing a musical theatre course has really inspired me to get these kids so that when they know they've got two auditions that day—one is for *South Pacific* and one's for *Rocky Horror*—they've got the facility to cope with those audition forms.

What role does voice science, or vocal anatomy and physiology, play in your work?

I think it's just essential. I don't talk in any form of imagery any more. All my students sit through videos. They've got to see what they're using, and if they don't, what's the point?

Do you use any recording equipment in your studio? Do you teach microphone techniques?

I absolutely teach microphone techniques. We have bare, basic equipment in our vocal studio. We can record on tape, a little bit of backing . . . I'm not really big into the MP3s and I'm certainly not big into recorded backing tracks.

So, in classes, are you working live most of the time?

Yes. We have a budget now for an accompanist to come in to all the major study classes twice a semester. But I'm a piano player and one of the other teachers is a player, so it makes it much easier, especially in contemporary jazz, for arranging, sorting out the keys, and going, "Oh let's do this and let's play with this and let's be inventive and let's reharmonize that." I find the other way too locked in. I hate backing tracks, and I hate karaoke.

Oh you're a person after my own heart!

Karaoke, single-handedly, has killed the music industry. I own a club and I think, "I need entertainment. I'll put in someone to play karaoke." The customers will keep themselves amused and it's costing me $50 a night. I put a band in, that's costing me $500.

And you train the public to expect less.

Sure. The true solo artist comes along and the club manager says, "Well, where are all your MP3s, where are your backing tracks, and where's your band in the box?" So this poor singer has to go out and pay hundreds of dollars for equipment and download this rubbish off the Internet. It's about as creative as my cat!

I teach microphone techniques because that's part of the industry now, and the hardest thing for the classical students is to use microphones. And for the contemporary students, the sound system is now a part of what they do; it's a part of their embellishment. We actually do workshops on microphones, the types of microphones to buy, the difference between radio microphones and cardioid or condenser microphones and dynamic microphones. They know how to set their own sound up, and that's important.

THE TRAINING

Where do you start? What are the vital signs you check right away when a student comes to you? What are the foundational aspects of training to which you regularly attend?

With a class, when I start at the beginning of the academic year, I don't know the students, the classical students especially. I don't know their voices and I don't know their voice range. So everyone has to do a presentation and they have to sing for me and tell me about what they've done. From there I start to outline what we'll be doing. The first thing I check is why the students are in this class. What do you want from this class, what do you need, what skills do you feel you need to upgrade? And because it's class-based, it's a different approach to a major study.

What do you expect to observe in a singer who is well trained or in a performer who sings well, with or without training?

I think physical awareness has got to be the first thing, so even if they're not formally trained, or if they've done training with a teacher somewhere along the line, that they're aware of the physicality, they're aware of the instrument, they know what makes the instrument work. Generally the students who come to me within the university itself will know physiologically what they're doing. They will know their voice, and yet they won't necessarily be well trained in a technique or approach.

Granted, the journey is different from one singer to another, but would you say something about how students might get from A to B, or from their first lessons—and I'm thinking individual lessons, but you can adapt this any way you like—from their first lessons with you to a solid professional technique?

Even in the class situation, I select a piece for them that I know will take them out of their comfort zone, and they also select a piece that perhaps they know. Then I will spend as much time as I possibly can over a couple of lessons to get them to research the character, bring it back and example it to me, even down to the physicalities of the accents. If they're doing something from *Sweeney Todd*, then I don't want an American accent; I want British. If they're doing any intrinsic American show, then why are you saying *cahn't?*

I love what you're saying, Lisa. Change the accent and you've changed the world of that character, the body, the physicality, everything.

Right, and as I keep saying to everyone, accents are not just the sound; accents are physical. If you watch an American movie and then watch how we speak in an Australian movie, you're going to see great physical differences with the jaw and the tongue and the mouth, and that's what accents are about. But it's also part of what the character is about. So if they're from the Midwest, why do they speak that way? What are the social influences? One young girl who's doing Adelaide now didn't know how to get that accent. She was doing all this damage. So I said, "No, come on." We got the physicality of it going, then the sound, and all of a sudden the voice was just floating into it.

In the answers to earlier questions, you have touched on some, if not all, of the six aspects of training listed below:

Alignment, Breathing, Range, Resonance, Articulation, Connection (the Acting Dimension)

Now, from the perspective of your own approach, will you comment specifically on each of these technical elements, to whatever extent and in whatever order you choose?

Well, obviously the first two on the list are the first two I will look at, their *breathing* and *alignment*, because often in musical theatre, you're being asked to do some perhaps unusual things, and if you're not aligned and if your breathing is not under control, you're not going to achieve the right *resonance* and *range*. So those become very prominent in the early stages of the training and then we're going into *articulation*, especially in regard to accents. I find sometimes with the classical singers that their articulation is very poor. And then you get to the *connection*, and you're going, "But this song is a continuation of the script," so if you said to your lover, "I'm going to kill myself," and then you sing this song and I can't understand what you're saying about *how* you're going to kill yourself—I don't know if you're going to poison yourself, shoot yourself, or jump off a building—you've got to articulate that really clearly, and that's when we go into the speech quality side of things.

Again, from your perspective, how do these individual aspects of training relate to one another (1) in the learning process, and then, (2) in performance?

To me they're obvious in the learning process, in the craft-based process, so that by the time they get to the performance those craft-based techniques are part of what they're doing and the communication of the performance becomes everything.

Do you have additional comments you'd like to make?

I suppose I've always been a bit of a rebel and that's gotten me into trouble, but now I figure I'm too old to change, so I'll just go along that way! At the end of the day you're gonna go, "Hey, it's okay, I can go now because I've followed the path that I chose to follow, not someone else's path." Whether or not I've achieved everything I wanted to achieve is not the question. It's "I've followed the path that I needed to follow; I haven't followed your path, I've followed mine."

DISCS

Lisa Ryan-McLaughlin. 2003. *Compilation: The Jazz Queensland Collection.* Brisbane, Queensland. Merlo JQ001.

———. 2002. *Swing Like the Devil.* Brisbane, Queensland. McJazz MCD 006.

———. 2001. *The Nuclear Family: It's About Time.* Brisbane, Queensland. McJazz MCD 011.

———. 2000. *Mus'n'Touch: Defending The Groove*. Brisbane, Queensland. MTCD 008.

———. 1999. *Compilation: The Great Tropical Jazz Party*. Townsville, Queensland. JPCD003.

11. Jason Barry-Smith

Jason Barry-Smith walked over to meet me following a rehearsal at Queensland Conservatorium. As I entered the lobby of the hotel, I thought, "How will I know Jason?" We'd communicated via e-mail, but without arranging clues for recognition. No worry though! It was easy to spot this handsome young actor/singer by the ease of his movement and the warmth of his manner.

Photography by Kenji Photography

Jason Barry-Smith is one of Australia's most sought-after singers. He has performed a huge range of repertoire, including the title role in the Australian premiere of Billy Budd; *Enjolras in* Les Miserables *(Wellington Operatic); Major General Stanley in* The Pirates of Penzance *(Essgee Productions); Morales and Dancaire in* Carmen *(Opera Queensland); the title role of* Don Giovanni, *for which he won a National Opera Award (Opera Queensland); Tony in* West Side Story *for the Brisbane River Festival; and the Birdseller in* Sweeney Todd, *Dr. Malatesta in* Don Pasquale, *and Christian in* Un Ballo in Maschera, *all for Opera Queensland. In addition, he is in high demand as one of Brisbane's most respected singing teachers, specializing in classical and music theatre repertoire.*

PERSPECTIVE

Would you say something about your background and about what influenced or informed your approach to teaching?

I did a lot of work in popular music as a young kid. Then when I went through high school I became more and more serious and got interested in classical music. Then I went to the conservatorium and graduated with a bachelor of music. I also started postgraduate studies in opera but didn't totally finish it because gigs started coming in. When I graduated, I started looking at going into music theatre because I knew I wasn't quite ready to go into operatic repertoire. I have a lyric baritone voice, which has grown since then, but at the time it was a very light sound and I thought that there was music theatre repertoire that I could explore and use to gain experience. I find the eight months just after I graduated and before I got my first good gig most fascinating in hindsight. I wasn't singing much, I was getting depressed about it, and I found that I was not really singing particularly well. Finally, I came to a point when I thought, "This is ridiculous. Okay, I'm going to take charge and I'm going to re-look at *why* I'm singing, firstly, and then secondly, *how* one actually does it!" because for a long time I'd been singing with technique, but there had been no real thought process in what I was doing. This was a great watershed for me because from that point I realized that there was something more that I *needed* to know. It was then I discovered that I had a real passion for understanding physiologically what was happening with my technique.

The other thing that I became very passionate about when I started working in music theatre was the way everything is based on text. I was lucky because I did an exchange year in Munich Hochschule, which was fantastic. I worked with Professor Hanno Blaschke, who was the head of the vocal department at the time, and because my German wasn't that good, he put me with what they called a diction specialist. This man was an actor who sang! It was absolute heaven because I got to work with this actor who knew all the classical repertoire for lyric baritone because he sang it as well. We worked on all of the big Schubert song cycles, the Schumann song cycles; it was the most incredible experience. So that just linked me into this whole thing of the text being the driving force. It doesn't mean that you can't make a beautiful sound while you're getting the text across, but it just has to be an appropriate sound for that type of music.

Do you work with students on classical as well as musical theatre repertoire?

I do. And I must say that it is at times more frustrating than music theatre because, especially for younger students, there is a feeling of distance, I guess you could call it, between the repertoire and where they are in their lives, whereas the music theatre repertoire is far more immediate for them to deal with. That's why I always get my classical students to sing music theatre repertoire as well, because they usually feel that they can open themselves up much more in that repertoire.

What about the other way round—if you are teaching someone who is focusing primarily on music theatre, do you have that student sing anything classical?

I do. There've been a couple of people with whom I've tried this with less than successful results, but it's always interesting. The things I find easiest to deal with are aria antiche. I normally use those to start with because they're not hugely difficult, and they get students to think in a more abstract way. Students are more able to focus on their tone and their sense of legato.

And sometimes they need that.

Absolutely, because there are lots of music theatre singers who get into problems because they don't have consistent support or line.

How would you describe the vocal requirements for singers in musical theatre today? How have those requirements changed over the years and where do you think they're going?

I think the vocal requirements are far greater in stylistic diversity, and that creates many problems, because at one stage, I guess up until around about the beginning of the sixties, we could all sing basically the same way. But then we started getting musicals that were rock musicals, pop musicals, and others that are more operatic in their conception. So really, most of the problems that I find with industry professionals today revolve around stylistic versatility. Those who sing very well in a music theatre style may not be able to sing something like *Staying Alive*, where everyone has to sound like the pop/rock singers of the 1970s. And even those who can bridge the style gap not only have to make that sound, but they're going to need to do it eight times a week and perform big dance numbers at the same time. I've found that the more they go back to their legitimate music theatre technique, the more longevity they have. To be quite honest, it's more about doing different phrasings and articulations than trying to create a new sound that makes the difference. If there is something that's more legitimately operatic, you need to concentrate more on the sense of the line and the legato than, necessarily, on changing what you are doing physiologically. I think making stylistic changes rather than large technical adjustments is more successful in these situations because people don't get confused. They don't start creating problems that they don't need to have.

That's a very interesting perspective. What role does voice science, or vocal anatomy and physiology, play in your work with students or clients?

There are really only two basic things that I focus on with beginning students: dealing with breathing—making sure that what's set up is not collapsing all of the time; and then, making sure that registration doesn't get too thick. They're two things that I really get very finicky about in the beginning stages. When singers begin to understand that registration is not about pitches, that it's all about muscular changes at the vocal folds, it can be like scales falling from their eyes. I think that knowing that the body is basically just a big complicated machine, and that the parts that we focus on when singing are just movable parts within that machine, allows them to have a sense of the whole machine working together, once coordination skills become more and more habitual.

Does movement or movement-based training play a role in your teaching?

Yes. I'm a yoga person myself and I absolutely adore what it can achieve. We also had a fantastic lecturer at the conservatory, Anna Sweeney, [whose] focus was on allowing the body to be something that actually *enhances* what you are doing vocally, rather than hindering it.

I love that! It's so obvious but . . .

It seems so obvious, doesn't it?

Do you teach microphone techniques?

I do teach microphone techniques, because I think that that's something everybody should be very aware of, especially opera singers. I know so many opera singers who are frightened of microphones. Music theatre singers are generally miked with bug mikes, but even so, there are going to be times for all singers when they're going to have to deal with a handheld mike. Lots of people have had awful experiences working with microphones, and the thing is, it's not rocket science. There just has to be a sense of ease with holding something and understanding what's needed from you to make the sound more consistent.

THE TRAINING

Where do you start? What are the foundational aspects of training to which you regularly attend?

Well, it's different depending on whether it is a beginning student or whether it's a student who is somewhat advanced in his or her career. With beginner students, one of the first things that I want to check is whether they really have the aptitude to switch on, because, truthfully, as a teacher, that is *the* most frustrating thing in the world. I want to see that if I say something to somebody, they are going to take it, process it, then do something about it. From that point on, we sing through something they feel comfortable doing and the things that I really look and listen for, I guess, are the postural things, whether the person is dealing with air in a way that seems structured, whether there is a consistent vocal sound, and whether there seem to be any problems that need to be dealt with immediately. They're the main things that I look for, as well as some type of musical ability, because, again, you can make pretty sounds, but if there's no concept of making music, that's a much harder thing to deal with.

What do you expect to observe in a singer who is well trained or in a performer who sings well, with or without training?

That the person allows me to join them in some sort of communion, because that, for me, is what it's all about. Every person achieves that in a different way, but I guess what we're all trying to do through training is create an effective communication with as much ease as possible, and without allowing the focus to be broken.

It's such a funny thing when you're on stage, or even when you are listening to a recording: There are times when it's very easy for the focus to drop. And that's when you start thinking about what you're going to buy at the supermarket later that day, rather than being taken on that journey. Good performers make it seem like it's never ending, and once you get to the end of it, you wish it could have gone on forever.

I was just thinking that that's the actor in you. I mean it's what the actor has to do.

Yes, and I think that a lot of performers forget that a performance is about more than just singing. So often I've been to a concert by a well-known artist and been let down by the bits in between the songs. I mean, during the songs they are glorious—confident and self-assured—but as soon as they have to string a couple of sentences together to introduce the next number, they lose it. And as an audience member, I find that disappointing. It's at those times that the magic stops for me.

Granted, the journey is different from one singer to another, but if you think it appropriate, would you cite a couple of examples of how students might get from A to B, or from their first lessons with you to a solid professional technique?

I think what students have to do right from the beginning, if they intend to have a professional career, is create some sort of practice régime that works, and that can be the thing that holds them back or moves them along. What I'd recommend is short amounts spaced throughout the day, but every day, six days a week. They can take a day off on Sunday or whatever, but basically short amounts of time so they don't get too caught up in listening to themselves and watching themselves and getting panicky about it. Then when they feel comfortable with their régime, we take time to renew it, setting new goals and challenges to keep the passion and momentum going. It's something that I try to do every six months or so when I'm dealing with people over long periods of time. That type of practice technique was never really taught to me when I was a student and I wish it had been.

In the answers to earlier questions, you have certainly touched on some, if not all, of the six aspects of training listed below:

Alignment, Breathing, Range, Resonance, Articulation, Connection (the Acting Dimension)

Now, from the perspective of your own approach, would you comment specifically on each of these technical elements, to whatever extent and in whatever order you choose?

Alignment. Where do you start, because it's about the whole thing really? And it's something that has to be in place before anything else really functions with a sense of ease. It is something that I am a tyrant about, which is terrible because you can see the students' eyes go, "Oh god, he's going to come over and start pulling at the back of my head or start saying, 'Oh you've locked your knees.' " But it is such an important aspect of the whole thing. I'm sure everyone has a different way of dealing with it, but for my students I've found that the easiest way is to give them a concept that starts from their feet and goes up. At each of the major points where there can be a problem, I give them a checklist to go through if they're having problems or feeling uneasy. The thing that I try to get them to do is make sure they've got a sense of their body being part of the performance, not just singing from the neck up.

Breathing. I've simplified my concept of breathing over a period of time. I think that most people, unless they have a big problem, do it pretty well themselves. I mean, breathing is a natural process that we do thousands of times per day without even thinking about it, but sometimes when we start talking about it and analyzing it, we get confused. I have met students who were taught the exact opposite of natural breathing, which is crazy, but I think the simpler you keep things as far as breathing goes, the better.

The other thing with breathing that interests me a lot is how you breathe for different phrases, because for each piece of text (I always come back to the text), there'll be a different way that singers would breathe if they were going to say that line. All of my students hate it when I get them to do it, but having them read the text before they start singing is something that I find very useful. Unfortunately, most students find it a bit uncomfortable, but, as I say to them, "You can't really sing a phrase with any sense of meaning unless you can *say* it with a sense of meaning as well."

Range. I used to read things in books about *building vocal range* and it always filled me with trepidation because I had a lyric voice that sat quite high and I never had to worry about building a range. So I used to think, "Oh gosh, if I didn't have to do it, how am I going to teach other people?" And then I realized that when the voice functions easily, the range comes. So I concentrate on getting the vocal production as easy as possible: making sure the whole body is being used, that the breath is working, and that registration is not getting too heavy, specifically in music theatre singers. I think that's something that female singers, especially, have to really concentrate on, because in a lot of pieces written now, they're expected to go right over that changeover point and not sound like they're making a huge gear change. It really is the female voice that has gone through the greatest change. What I've found, especially with the beautiful writing for women by Jason Robert Brown, is that he finds far more *expressive* range through using greater vocal range. I also think Sondheim was doing that in the seventies and eighties, but we had a time when perhaps the vocal technique of performers wasn't quite up to the challenges of what he was asking for. It's interesting comparing the original cast to the most recent recording of *Into the Woods.* God love Bernadette Peters! She is just stunning as the witch, but it's a far more effortful sound that Vanessa Williams is able to achieve. That doesn't preclude either of them being fantastic; we're just talking about vocal technique. But with the girls playing Cinderella, particularly, it's quite interesting to note the difference. The newer singer is a lot more savvy to the ways she can change over into that upper sound and back again but not sound operatic, and that's a lovely thing to hear.

Again, from your perspective, how do these individual aspects of training relate to one another (1) in the learning process and (2) in performance?

I think that we're much more aware of the individual facets of vocal production when we're in the studio. What we're trying to do within our learning and practice time is to try and make those facets as organic as possible; in other words, training our muscle memory so when we come to perform, we can concentrate more on the communication as a whole and forget about the nitty-gritty of technique. All too often, with young singers, you see their technique on their face, and I find that really detracts from an enjoyable performance.

On the weekend I had to take my brother-in-law to the hospital and we were there until 2:30 in the morning, my wife and I. Then the next night I was singing a performance and during the day I was thinking, "I've got to do a show tonight, I've got to do a show tonight." And so when I got to the theatre I was freaking out! "Oh gosh I was out late last night, oh I was out late last night." That was the last thing I needed to think of. Finally, in the wings I had a good talking to myself, got focused on the job at hand, and did one of my best shows of the season. The technique, if it's allowed to, just kicks in and lets you fly.

I guess those sorts of things happen to everybody, but we have to remember that, ultimately, Mr. and Mrs. General Public won't want to know about them. They don't want to know what the process has been for you to get to that point. All they want to know is that they are having a fantastic time, and they don't want to be taken out of that moment. As soon as I see a person thinking about technique on stage I'm lost, I switch off—it's terrible, but I just do. Hopefully, that's partly what that question was about.

Yes, it was indeed. Do you have additional comments you'd like to make?

Not really. I think I've spoken quite at length about a lot of things, all of which probably surround one basic concept: It all has to end up being a performance.

RECORDINGS

Barry-Smith, J. 2005. Soloist, Ariel Ramirez's *Misa Criolla* and *Navidad Nuestra*. Brisbane: The Queensland Youth Choir.

———. 2003. The Boatswain, Gilbert and Sullivan's *HMS Pinafore*. Sydney: Essgee Productions. Video 1997, ABC Classics; DVD reissue 2003, ABC Classics.

12. Debbie Phyland

Photography by Joey Phyland

The following day I flew to Melbourne, where Debbie Phyland was my contact and gracious hostess. Almost immediately upon arriving, I saw The Producers, *which Debbie had coached. Then, as with Wendy LeBorgne in Cincinnati, I was privileged to observe a day in the clinic with this gifted young speech pathologist/voice specialist. In the evening we attended a production of Tom Scott's* The Daylight Atheist *(Melbourne Theatre Company), which was vocally stunning, as it required Richard Piper's excursion into every nook and cranny of extended voice use. Debbie had served as a consultant on the show.*

Debbie Phyland is a speech-language pathologist/researcher, musical theatre performer and vocal coach, and a teacher whose work encompasses many dimensions of voice use. We met in Sydney at the Australian National Association of Teachers of Singing (ANATS) Symposium in mid-July of 2004, and the following interview was recorded at her practice, Voice Medicine Australia, in East Melbourne.

PERSPECTIVE

Would you say something about your background and about what influenced or informed your approach to teaching?

I am a speech pathologist and so completed my bachelor of applied science for speech pathology as an undergraduate, which is the way we do it in Australia, for four years. Then I worked in the acute hospital setting for twelve years, working predominantly with ENT issues, head and neck cancers, and neurology. During that time I was also performing as a professional singer in music theatre and cabaret. Then I completed a master's degree by research, looking at the epidemiology of voice problems among singers. The focus was surveying music theatre, classical, and contemporary singers and looking at what some of their risk factors were. I completed the master's about eight years ago and had been working in voice before that time, but had not really brought the two together. It was about ten years ago that my research became a catalyst for bringing my love and passion for performing into the speech path arena. It was really only then that I started working in this area, left my acute hospital position, and became focused on working in voice clinics and in the laryngology field. So my background is twofold. It's as a speech pathologist with a keen interest and experience in voice, and then as a performer. Because my background is very much in cabaret and music theatre, I think that's allowed me to follow my nose with those clients.

Do you work with students on classical as well as musical theatre repertoire? Do you teach vocal styles other than classical and musical theatre?

Although I certainly work with the classical singers, I'm less inclined to get into "fixing things that ain't broke," and I'm less inclined to be as instructional with that technique as I would be with music theatre. Certainly, if there were overt signs of technical issues, I'd be likely to make comment on that, but I have the luxury of having a number of excellent singing teachers in town that I would rely on to work on those angles.

Do I teach vocal styles? Well, sort of, yes. I work a lot with jazz singers, pop or contemporary rock, R&B, and Australian singing, which is a bit similar to country and western but has its own vocal flavor, and it's particularly bold. It's probably a little bit brassy; it can rely on some belt and yet it's got a different style. The genres are fairly broad, and although I under-stand and reinforce the influence of musical genre on voice production, I also have a general sense of a model, if you like, of vocal efficiency, which is my starting point. So the vocal style may not be particularly different in terms of the mechanics and the physiology, but the interpretation and the way that's used, and the vocal line may be very different. So, yes, I do work with other styles but I don't teach from a style-specific orientation.

How would you describe the vocal requirements for singers in musical theatre today? How have those requirements changed over the years and where do you think they're going?

At the moment in Melbourne, and in Australia in general, there's a really strong flavor of rock musicals, so we've had *We Will Rock You*, we've had *Rent, Mamma Mia, Urinetown* (although that is more of a spoof of other styles), but certainly the rock musicals have been very, very big over the last few years. And that has had a big impact, I think, on the vocal requirements for singers, particularly in terms of their vocal load. A lot of them have come from a pop/rock background, rather than a music theatre background, and they're trying to survive eight shows a week, so that creates all sorts of issues for them in terms of longevity and endurance. The classical, light operatic voice is really not getting as much work at present. Singers need to have that vocal versatility and flexibility as per-formers to cross a range of vocal styles. Without that, they're not going to be able to get work.

I think, in Australia, we have changed from regularly casting "dancers who sing"; we are getting singers who are really good singers, who are get-ting employed in their own right as singers—and, hopefully, they can also dance—whereas probably ten years ago you were much more likely to get the dancing singers and the acting singers. So the vocal requirements of singers have increased. They definitely need to belt, but in a really rocky sense. The operetta-style voice is not as needed in musical theatre and so we don't have many of those old traditional musicals. The Australian image is still emerg-ing in music theatre and we are regularly called upon to create the Broadway sound, in terms of the particularly brassy, sassy, sort of twangy sound. And I think that we are getting better at producing it, that Australian singers traditionally weren't good at that because they were not used to having that really focused "nyaaa." We tend to produce a lazier, broader sound.

Where we're going I don't know. I think we're getting more and more comfortable with the Australian sound, and I think the Australian audiences are becoming much more receptive to Australian stories being told in musical format. We've had the likes of *Boy from Oz* and other ones you may or may not have heard of that have been emerging. There's one, *Eureka*, that opens soon and is characteristic of new shows telling our heritage, which is really exciting for Australia. Here our vocal identity embraces our multicultural background but becomes defined in its own right because we are no longer having to emulate the American pop sound, or even assume the traditional British operetta sound, as for Gilbert and Sullivan. Gilbert and Sullivan is often being enjoyed in Australia now if it's very spoofed and hammed up to a point that it becomes caricatured or taken to the absolute parody extreme (almost a bit vaudevillish). Cabaret is the main musical theatre trend at present and has replaced most of the theatre restaurant performances, aiming for more intimacy and following a narrative form.

Why do you teach what you teach? What is your passion in this work?

I teach what I teach because I feel very strongly about vocal health. I have a very strong physiological model, so my teaching methods are very inspired by my thirst, or curiosity, for understanding the mechanism. I *love* the troubleshooting; I *love* trying to change something at a scientific level, and I love the fact that that usually makes a better sound aesthetically. I am intrinsically a scientist, and so what drives me is the fact that I get to combine two areas of my life: my art and my scientific hat. This way the two meet completely, hopefully, or symbiotically, which is great. And my passion in this work is definitely for the art; my passion is the fact that sound is exciting and that sound excites and ruminates within me, and that when I get a perfect balance in resonance from somebody, then I find that that makes me resonate.

Do you use any recording equipment in your studio?

Yes, I do, but not for the usual purposes. I use it for feedback, just so that the singer can get the value of listening. I find that one of my main issues is that singers are often used to listening to themselves, and they're not used to feeling, so I really rely a lot more on kinesthetic stuff. I've become less reliant on auditory feedback than I used to be. I also rely on the recording for my own accountability. As a baseline, I usually do a recording because, again, the scientist in me likes to have the potential to then evaluate that acoustically, if I need to. Having said that, I rarely do acoustic analysis for time reasons. I have quite a commitment to going through a recording repertoire initially to make sure that I've got all that as a database for future evaluation.

THE TRAINING

Where do you start? What are the vital signs you check right away when a student comes to you? What are the foundational aspects of training to which you regularly attend?

Where I start is always with listening. Listening before anything, probably even before watching. I am listening to the *vocal efficiency*, which is, I suppose, a sort of laboratory term, but I'm also appreciating the *vocal production* as my first step. I'm really looking to see whether they're being as efficient as they can be: how much extraneous effort is being required to produce that sound, whether or not it's balanced. Before looking at a performance, I start with the voice.

In terms of resonance?

Definitely in terms of resonance, but mostly in terms of vocal quality, which is, I believe, different from resonance in terms of vocal fold efficiency or competency of laryngeal valving. So I think I'm inherently a speech pathologist, where we get stuck at the glottal level, so the vibratory patterns probably start me off. I want to know how well those vocal folds are vibrating, and I think also about the resonance and the subglottic aspects, like breathing, all of that. I suspect that I'm overly preoccupied with that, but I feel that if the supraglottic and subglottic resonance is good, the larynx and tongue position appropriate, and the breathing's right, then the vocal fold vibration will be very efficient and that will tell me a lot. I've never thought about where I start. I think I just follow their lead. I think I'd listen to the noisiness of the signal. I think I'm very focused, usually, on what that sound production is like. Then all the other stuff I see as maybe being the reason that sound is like that.

What do you expect to observe in a singer who is well trained
or in a performer who sings well, with or without training?

Flexibility, vocal flexibility, so the ability to use their voice flexibly, the ability to access their full range, their full dynamic pitch range and intensity range, the ability to create a sound that is effortless and without unnecessary tensions. I expect a sound to excite me, and I'd expect the performance to communicate to me. In terms of singing well, with or without training, I would expect their sound to make me think cognitively that they were as efficient as they could be, that they were doing things that were proportionate and were healthy. I think I would feel that they were inherently healthy vocally and that they could last the distance.

Granted, the journey is different from one singer to another,
but if you think it appropriate, would you cite a couple of examples
of how students might get from A to B, or from their first lessons
with you to a solid professional technique?

I'll give you one example, first, of the most common way in which I become involved. When I go into Melbourne Theatre Company and listen to the company's first read, I might hear in someone's vocal quality that they were in trouble, that they were hyperfunctional, so, for example, I would hear glottal attacks. I would hear that there's a noise in the sound source, and that there was evidence of quite significant tension in the neck, that is, hyperfunction. Then there's a process whereby I would talk to that person, firstly, about whether or not that was their habitual posture, their laryngeal position, or whether they think this is their voice normally. They may have been cast because of that quality, or there may have been a significant event in their lives just prior to going into a show, jeopardizing their vocal health. In this particular case of a girl I'm thinking of, who was cast in a lead role in the production of *Company*, she was cast for her particular voice quality. She was someone who was relatively dysphonic and was quite anxious; it was her first professional gig in a while. The first step was to help her get some awareness that it was safe to improve her voice production, and that although she'd been cast for the huskiness, I wasn't going to get rid of any of that special quality, but was trying to make it safer or easier for her to vocalize eight times a week. So the journey involved the two of us becoming calibrated in terms of our sense of her identity and my perspective of what was going to cause her grief. We made sure we were aligned first and that we had a common agenda, or goal, which was to improve her endurance and efficiency without changing anything that was essential. Then, in that journey, it was a case of giving her some exercises that I felt would balance her vocal production a bit better. For example, specific isotonic, isometric exercises and drills six times a day—although I was relatively certain her vocal folds were edematous and it was counterproductive to assess this. The drills were specifically targeting the reduction of potential edema and for the purpose of just improving muscle memory and reinforcing efficient voicing. Then I worked specifically on the material and helped her to perform some of those pitch changes, particularly in the breaks, that might have been tricky, and it might be a matter of just giving her some quick tricks. They would be quick fixes without changing the essence of her, just to say, "Okay, let's try that with a slightly different tongue position or larynx position, a different resonance." And particularly focusing on resonance, I'd be sure that the vocal identity she'd interpreted for the character was the best one for that character. I would work then with the music director and the director to make sure they were happy because we shifted her interpretation of that character. In this example, we shifted off the larynx, so rather than make this character vocally hyperfunctional, we made the character subtly different. The performer felt she'd found a new voice without losing her own vocal identity. I suppose it's about working quite carefully on giving her a safer spot to go for that character that was also safe for her psychologically and easy for her to access. It had to be a quick fix because I've only got the luxury of a couple of sessions. And then at the end of that journey, I think she realized what she didn't know about her own voice. After the season she decided to explore a lot more about her voice and her understanding. She developed much more as a performer and linked up with a really good singing teacher to continue her vocal development.

In the answers to earlier questions, you have certainly touched on some, if not all, of the six aspects of training listed below:

Alignment, Breathing, Range, Resonance, Articulation, Connection (the Acting Dimension)

Now, from the perspective of your own approach, would you comment specifically on each of these technical elements, to whatever extent and in whatever order you choose?

I'll start with *resonance* because I think that when the resonance is balanced and appropriate to the source, reciprocal with the source in terms of the resulting excellent resonance quality, that all the other is usually pretty spot-on. So I see that as the ultimate outcome, but also the beginning. So when the sound is as resonant as it can be, whether that be light, bright, brassy, dark, whatever, it probably means there've been adjustments to the other areas that have allowed that to happen. I feel that resonance and vocal quality are reciprocal. I see vibratory characteristics, or vocal fold source vibrations, as being highly dependent on resonance, and vice versa, so that if the vocal fold vibration is aperiodic or inefficient, then we'll be able to hear that in the resonance; no matter how hard we work supraglottically or subglottically, we are not going to be able to get the quality of the sound we want. And vice versa—that if we haven't got the placement right, then it's going to be very hard to get those vocal folds to just flap in the wind. So, resonance, I think, is crucial.

Alignment is almost assumed in my work, but often incorrectly assumed. Unless there's an obvious issue there, that is not a particularly strong aspect of my approach.

I like *breathing* to look after itself, unless it's really obvious, but I work a lot on the intake, in the sense of—again, stuck in the vocal fold level—audible inhalations are one of the things I most commonly change. Two things I commonly change: one's hard glottal attacks; the second is audible inhalations. I also work on breathing for promotion of breath control subglottically. I use aspects of an Accent Method approach. I love going back to some basics of changing subglottic pressure for the purpose of voicing, and getting them to do those efficiently as possible once I'm confident they control airflow with ease and balance. Breathing, for voicing (coordination, control, release), I do often need to work on, but only if I've got their resonance in a good spot and their vocal fold vibration is periodic or competent. The breathing will often look after itself as long as the inspirations aren't audible. The exhalation is also important but in conjunction with timing for voicing. So my focus on breathing's probably more to do with timing than how to *breathe*, but still making sure that they are getting the right amount of breath in.

Articulation in music theatre is really crucial, and I spend a lot of time on tongue position, because I find in Australia we have a real tendency, particularly when we do an American accent, to adopt a backed tongue posture, so we have to be careful not to develop tongue root tension. I may provide exercises, for example, to provide tongue/jaw independence or improved consonant precision.

Range I rarely work on as an agenda, but I would presume that by making singers more efficient, their range improves. Range, in the sense of being able to cross over styles, yes—their flexibility, versatility, and their agility are really important to me. I rarely try and get them to extend their pitch range unless it's an obvious issue. I do, however, commonly work a lot on the passaggio, in terms of helping them to sometimes go into the swap-over registers.

What about the acting dimension?

Absolutely. *Connection* is crucial, in the context of connection with the character and themselves and their interpretation of themselves in that character, particularly in the sense of how they find the voice for that character. How much is them and how much is something they've created and assumed? I try to make them realize it's in their own repertoire; it doesn't need to be assumed. So vocal authenticity is really crucial. Connection is about authenticity and emotional connection, which will ensure connection with breath, phonation, the text, the context, and with the other performers.

Again, from your perspective, how do these individual aspects of training relate to one another (1) in the learning process and (2) in performance?

I think alignment, breathing, and articulation are fundamental to the performance and need never to be thought of again. In the learning process, they are the stepping-stones, but once they're solid, they need to be assumed. I think resonance and range are things that can change very dynamically and the first things that I see disappear in a performance are resonance and range (in terms of accessibility to loud and soft and high and low), particularly if performance anxiety sets in and then the connection is lost. I would really want to make sure they had a very strong sense of where they were going to place that sound, and how to keep it there, and to remind them of that place when they warm up or in their preparation for performance. Then if they are totally connected with their character, all of those other areas are the sub-skills, so that they can then concentrate ultimately on the connection.

Do you have additional comments you would like to make?

I think it's a very vulnerable position to be in, to be someone working with voice, because with where we're at now, there's a huge level of accountability. I think it's scared off some very good, intuitive, perceptive teachers. I think there are people who know how to create sounds that are terrific, but may not have a good understanding of physiology, and I think it's important that we don't devalue that perception and intuition. Teachers have been getting increasingly more accountable for pedagogical understanding, and that is critical, but the ear is still fundamental to a teacher. I never cease to be amazed at how two people can approach one person's performance completely differently and effect the same change, so that what you might do, Joan, and what I might do, might come from totally different directions. But in a master class like we saw last weekend, I thought, "Oh, that's an interesting way of doing it," and it wouldn't have been what I might have done, but I think I would have got a similar change. So I don't think the method is as crucial as the outcome. My point is that if the sound is beautiful and moves us, then our method has been spot-on. If the sound jars us or has an effect on us that's negative, if it distracts us or makes us lose contact with that person, then we've probably not used the right method.

Brilliant! Thank you so much, Debbie.

SELECTED PUBLICATIONS

Holmes, R., Oates, J., Phyland, D., & Hughes, A. 2000. "Voice Characteristics in the Progression of Parkinson's Disease." *International Journal of Language and Communication Disorders* 35: 407–418.

Lim, W. P. C., Oates, J. M., Phyland, D. J., & Campbell, M. J. 1998. "Effects of Laryngeal Endoscopy on the Vocal Performance of Young Adult Females with Normal Voices." *Journal of Voice* 12, no. 1: 68–77.

Phyland, D. J. 1997. "The Speech Pathologist's Scope: Use of Endoscopy for the Evaluation of Voice and Swallowing." *Australian Communication Quarterly* 25, no. 1: 18–23.

——. 2005. "Voice Smarter Not Harder." *Australian Communication Quarterly* 7, no. 2: 61–63.

Phyland, D. J., Oates, J., & Greenwood, K. 1999. "Self-Reported Voice Problems among Professional Singers." *Journal of Voice* 13, no. 4: 602–611.

13. Jean Callaghan

Now in Sydney, I traveled by cab to Glebe for a dinner party at the home of Jean Callaghan, whom I'd met in Brisbane on my first visit to Australia. Dr. Callaghan and I had presented workshops back to back and attended each other's sessions during the Fifth Voice Symposium of Australia. Singing technique as an integral part of theatre voice training was then a relatively new focus for me and a lively topic among voice professionals in the

Photography by Keith Saunders

States. In Australia, however, the idea of integration was neither new nor extraordinary and Jean Callaghan had single-handedly developed that aspect of the actor-training program at the University of Western Sydney. Her groundbreaking book, Singing and Voice Science (*Singular/Thomson Learning, 2000*), had just been published.

Dr. Jean Callaghan is one of the most respected teachers and researchers in Australia; she is based in Sydney and freelances as a specialist in vocal performance and pedagogy. She was on the research and development team for Sing&See™ specialized computer software designed to provide acoustic feedback for singers, and she has sung professionally in Australia, England, and Germany. The following interview was recorded in her teaching studio above the main part of the house, to the accompaniment of spirited conversation and wonderful aromas from the kitchen below.

PERSPECTIVE

Will you say something about your background and about what influenced or informed your approach to teaching?

Gee, when you're as old as me, just about everything you've done influences it.

That's exactly the answer I would give!

Actually, I started singing myself from the age of about five and started formal training when I was about sixteen, the thinking at the time being that you waited till the voice was mature before you started. But I did a lot of singing anyway before I embarked on any training. My *work* training was as a secretary, and so I sang as a part-time thing, but did do quite a lot of performing. And I then had a break, which I largely put down to Joan Sutherland! Just when I really needed to be moving into being much more professional, first I had a baby, and then I heard a recording of Joan Sutherland when she had just got her first big break, and it caused me to feel totally hopeless. I thought, "I am never going to be as good as that," so I stopped. But something like seven years later I went with my then-husband to Perth. I had decided I couldn't bear being a secretary and I really needed to train for something where I could be a bit autonomous. So I decided I was going to do a degree in architecture, and I didn't have a matriculation, a university entrance. I had been doing a correspondence thing to get me a matriculation in New South Wales, but then we went to Western Australia and things were different. I discovered that to get into architecture you had to have a year in another faculty and then line up for a selection process. So I walked up to the music department and said, "I have these qualifications, I have the highest Trinity College diploma as a singer, and I'm dying to do music," and I was admitted to a bachelor of music. My idea was that I would do a year of that and then I would line up for architecture. But, of course, I got heavily into music but was interested more in musicology, so that degree was a bachelor of arts, with honors, in musicology. For the research dissertation I looked at writings on vocal technique, and that was really a start of an interest. Then I started a research master's degree in music and language, which is another continuing interest. Then I decided if I was ever going to be a performer, I just had to do that, so I went to England and did some further training and then worked for a couple of years with a German opera company.

Where did you study in England?

In London. I studied voice privately with Eric Vietheer, an Australian of German parentage who had himself trained in Germany, and worked regularly with language and vocal coaches. I'd always been interested in German music, really through a series of accidents, I think. When I was growing up in Sydney, music was strongly influenced by Jewish refugees from Europe. When I started school I had a teacher who was Viennese and used to teach us Schubert songs in German. And when my father first bought a gramophone, he bought the collection that went with it, recordings of opera and operetta, mostly tenors and much of it in German. Then as a young singer I was given a scholarship by the Schubert Society in Sydney and learnt a lot about Lieder from the musicians running that society. So I think German music was in my head and getting work in Germany was a logical step.

Where were you in Germany?

I was in Kiel, in the north of Germany. Came back to Australia, was doing some recital work and oratorio, and teaching. And then just as my private teaching had really become very busy, I took a half-time job at the University of Western Sydney, and then it became three-quarter time and then it became full time. And working with people in an actor training program was terrific for me because even back when I was first starting teaching, I used to earn money typing PhDs and books. And I typed a PhD on athletics training and said, "Ah, I think this is very applicable to singing." At the time, that sort of idea was pretty strange, but I've always thought that that kind of body learning is so important for singing. That's another recurring theme, which was reawakened by going to work in the actor training course because I worked very closely in a team of four people: with an acting teacher, a movement teacher, a spoken voice teacher, and me. The course included all those specific areas individually, but there was also work on how to bring it all together in performance.

That's a great idea, and I don't think it happens very often.

Yes, so we would have separate sessions with the students but also would do joint things, so when we had performance projects, we would all work on them.

And you would actually communicate with one another.

That's right, and at one stage we had a research project where we looked for common ground in our terminology, because a lot of the terminology, I think, stands between us.

Who were the students? Were they actors or musical theatre students, or both?

They were undergraduate students training to be actors, but we felt that singing was an important part of that, not *just* for music theatre. Initially, when I went there, there had only been a very little bit of singing and I took it seriously. It was a bit of a shock to some of the students and there was a bit of resistance. I used to say, "You'll be surprised that quite often actors are asked to sing. Think of Shakespeare comedies. Think of Brecht plays. So many things, but even if you never get asked to sing, just as an extended voice use, it's got to be useful to you." But it is amazing: A lot of them go into theatre in education troupes or form cooperatives devising their own work and there's very often singing in it. So very soon some of the skeptics graduated and I'd get these phone calls saying, "Jean, guess what?" So I think, yes, it was very valuable, and the main reason I'm not at the university any more is that they started cutting the hours for practical teaching and one of the first things the university administration decided was that actors didn't need singing training.

So something you started and developed has been done away with for budgetary reasons.

Oh, yes, economic rationalism, or *ir*rationalism as I like to call it.

So you've really been a pioneer.

I guess so, yes.

Do you work with students on classical as well as musical theatre repertoire?

I certainly do.

Do you teach vocal styles other than classical and/or musical theatre?

No, I don't teach any pop and I love jazz but I don't teach jazz because I think it's pretty specialized. But I certainly teach all classical styles, and

I teach music theatre from the sort of standpoint I've just been talking about, as kind of acting with the voice. I certainly think opera is like that, too, so for me, music theatre used to be Wagner and I still think that there's a continuum.

This is a loaded question for you, but what role does voice science, or vocal anatomy and physiology, play in your work with students or clients?

Well, that's funny. People tend to think that if you know anything about those things that you must be a terribly mechanistic kind of teacher, whereas I just think it's my responsibility as a voice teacher to know how it works. That doesn't mean I'm going to talk in mechanistic or anatomical terms to students, but to have a diagnostic ear is vital. It's always been recognized that to teach voice, spoken or sung, one needs a very keen ear, and part of that is knowing what is producing what kind of effect. So if you don't know how it works in terms of the physiology and what the anatomical bits are doing, it's a bit of a guessing game, and I think that's unfair to students. Sometimes it can take a while to work out what's happening and how it can be improved, changed, or whatever, but sometimes there's a very simple answer and I think it's unfair to make a mystery of things like how you produce an /i/ vowel. I've sometimes seen that kind of mystery created in singing master classes.

Oh, yes.

Now the reality is, of course, that some students don't react terribly well to "Put your tongue here," but I think the teacher needs to know. And for most of them, yes, it's much simpler to say, "Put your tongue there."

Does movement or movement-based training (for example, the Alexander Technique, Feldenkrais, Pilates, or yoga) play a role in your teaching?

Very much so, not that I present myself as an expert, but I have done some training in *all* of those things, workshops in Alexander, Feldenkrais, Pilates, and ongoing yoga for years now, for myself. The body awareness and the *principles* certainly inform what I do. When I was at the university I could work from the knowledge that students were getting bodywork; now in private practice I certainly advocate that clients do some bodywork.

THE TRAINING

Where do you start? What are the vital signs you check right away when a student comes to you? What are the foundational aspects of training to which you regularly attend?

Vital signs, well, I check whether they're alive, which sometimes comes into question because they appear not to be breathing. I always have a consultation lesson with singers and the first thing I want to do is to hear them sing, and because they might have come from work or whatever, the first thing we do is a warm-up. If they have been with another teacher or have had some training, I will ask them what they've done, so I'll get some kind of idea what sort of routine they go through. And then I hear them sing, and when they sing, I'll be watching to see what the body alignment is like; that would be the most vital sign, how the body is being used. That sounds a self-evident and easy thing, but how we use ourselves, to use Alexander's term—what people might know in their heads and what they habitually do—are so often two different things. So I would be watching for the alignment and body use, breath management, what's happening at the larynx, and what's happening with the resonance. Of course, I'm also noticing whether things are musically good or not, I mean accurate or not, but also whether there's any musicality, any feeling being conveyed, any phrasing. I'd also be checking for speech or vocal problems. So I would be listening and watching for all those things, and then talking to the person and saying, "I perceive this, and what do you think?" I'm looking for a starting point, I guess. I look for something to hook onto, to build on, something that they can already do and then incorporate, trying to fix things that aren't right.

I would tend to start with stretching first, moving onto things to get the breathing mechanism going, things to get the articulatory bits working, making noises to move throughout the range. And then I would start applying those kind of things to musical patterns, technical exercises, not always scales. My aim would be to move through the whole range so that that's accessible for singing songs, and to sing different vowels and deal with registration, the lot really, and then move on to applying the vocal skills to songs. Yes, technical things but also, "What is this about?" "How are you conveying it?" "Say me the song text as a monologue." "Where is the climax in this song?" "What is the person thinking there?" "I don't understand what you're saying there," and so forth.

What do you expect to observe in a singer that is well trained or in a performer who sings well, with or without training?

I would expect the body to be working as well as the voice. I mean the body *is* the voice, but I wouldn't expect to see or hear vocal strain; I would expect to see a very active body. I would expect communication, with the words and with the music and with the vocal tone. I would expect a sensitivity to the text. So the music and the verbal text should fit together as one text and if they don't, a singer's got to make a decision about whether to go with the music or the words to make the performance meaningful. Or, if there is meant to be, as one of my former colleagues used to say, a "contrapuntal clash," then that should be brought out.

Granted, the journey is different from one singer to another, but would you say something about how students might get from A to B, or from their first lessons with you to a solid professional technique?

I guess one of the difficulties of teaching this kind of work is that the performer needs to know it as a Gestalt, but before you get to that, you have to teach the bits, and in teaching the bits, it tends to pull apart. I need to teach the bits and then help the singer find ways to put it together as chunks, and then bigger and bigger chunks, and then find the thought or impulse or movement that puts the chunks together in a sequence. I think that's one reason that I, along with a lot of other singing teachers, emphasize what you do on the in-breath. It's not the air so much; it's all the other things you do. The breath motivates the thought and it's all one movement, and as you take the breath you're activating the body, you're preparing the resonance, you have the thought in your head, and the thought includes all aspects of the music, including the color of it and the shape of the phrase—all those things. So I suppose the difference between the beginner and the experienced professional, or even the beginning professional, is that the beginner still has to consciously think about all those things, whereas they become an ingrained part of the expression of a professional singer, and professional singers often can't talk very rationally about those things. As a teacher, I think you have to be able to, but singers need to be able to do it by a thought, a feel, a kinesthetic memory. They need to know enough that if it goes wrong, they've got strategies for fixing it, but certainly you don't go out performing at a high level thinking,

"What's my jaw doing?" or "Where am I going to take a breath?" So I guess that's the journey. And if you're called in on a show, if you're working primarily with actors who are not really used to singing, a lot of it is convincing them that they continue to be actors when they sing. And while singing might be acting writ large, it's basically the same process.

In the answers to earlier questions, you have touched on some, if not all, of the six aspects of training listed below:

Alignment, Breathing, Range, Resonance, Articulation, Connection (the Acting Dimension)

Now, from the perspective of your own approach, will you comment specifically on each of these technical elements, to whatever extent and in whatever order you choose?

I think I'd say those were the basic aspects of singing and the only way I guess I would elaborate is to say, particularly if they're not full-time performers, that they need to pay attention to these things in daily life. Or if you're dealing with somebody who dances, you have to deal with the fact that the kind of breathing, and alignment for that matter, that they need to support some kinds of dance, may not be appropriate to the kind of singing they need to do. I always ask potential clients whether they have done any dance, movement, sport, to try and tap into habitual things, but also just their way of thinking.

Range. I try to develop the whole of the range and integral to that is dealing with registration because a lot of people, if they haven't sung, think their voice ends where their speaking voice ceases to work.

Resonance? Yes, vital, so a lot of talk about what you do with pharynx and palate and tongue and lips and all those things, and, of course, that's linked to *articulation.* And I think that's one of the hard things about singing because those are interrelated things. Now I think that is different from speaking—in singing it's much more exaggerated than in speech.

Perhaps, but with dialects, it's all there. It is all *integrated.*

So, yes, I work quite a lot on that. I think, in classical music, the resonance is predominant, whereas in a lot of music theatre styles, hearing the words may be more important.

Connection yes. To me, all of those things relate to the connection, and to what I was saying about the words and the music and the body being the text.

You really beautifully answered this question before when you were talking about the Gestalt and the need to focus on the pieces, but if there's anything you want to add, again from your perspective, how do these individual aspects of training relate to one another (1) in the learning process and (2) in performance?

In the learning process I'd be aiming to make singers aware of all these things and give them some techniques for actually working them. I laughed at myself when I was at the university when I produced a piece of paper called, "How to Learn a Song." But it did make me think about it and it's been used by other people since then, because I think a lot of people haven't really thought about it: how you need to focus on the bits and learn them, and then put it back together. So that would include learning the words and then learning them as a monologue. That said, I have to say I think when you memorize something, the music and the words go together and occasionally when I've had desperate time on stage, thinking, "I don't know what the next word is," when I've opened my mouth to sing, the word comes with the music. And that for me is the transition. It becomes very much just what you do to express yourself when you're onstage, rather than a conscious thing, but conscious enough if one gets into trouble.

Do you have additional comments you would like to make?

I don't think so. I'll think of them over dinner.

SELECTED PUBLICATIONS

Bartlett, I., Winkworth, A., & Callaghan, J. 2002. "Voice and Performance Profiles of Working Contemporary Commercial Singers: Implications for Voice Care." *Australian Voice* 8: 68–71.

Callaghan, J., & McDonald, E. 2003. "The Singer's Text: Music, Language and the Expression of Meaning." *Australian Voice* 9: 42–48.

Callaghan, J., & Mitchell, R. 2001. "Singing in Actor Training." *Australian Voice* 7: 23–30.

Callaghan, J., & Wilson, P. 1998. "My Life in Music and Research." In *Women and Non-Traditional Research: The Alternative Trek*, 1–7. Edited by N. Lengkeek & E. Deane. Sydney: Academic Development & Flexible Learning Unit, UWS Nepean.

Australian Association for Research in Music Education in *Advaning Music Education in Austrailia*, edited by David Forrest, 8–12. Parkville, Victoria: Australian Society of Music Education, 1999.

———. 2004. *Sing&See*™ software and accompanying manual, *How to Sing and See: Singing Pedagogy in the Digital Era*. Sydney: Cantare Systems.

Howes, P., Callaghan, J., Davis, P., Kenny, D., & Thorpe, W. 2004. "The Perception of Vibrato in Western Operatic Singing: Its Relationship to Measured Vibrato Onset, Rate, and Extent, Listener Preference, and Emotional Expression." *Journal of Voice* 18, no. 2: 216–230.

Web site: http://users.bigpond.net.au/CallaghanSingingVoice/

14. PAT WILSON

Pat Wilson is one of the most delightful human beings I have ever known. We "met" via e-mail as I was planning to come to Australia, then exchanged books, and finally met face to face at the home of Jean Callaghan soon after Pat's return from a national conference in New Zealand, where she had been a keynote speaker.

Photography by Stuart Campbell Photography, Australia

Pat Wilson is a multitalented performer who has worked as a singer, jazz pianist, composer, lyricist, actress, theatre critic, singing teacher, and music director in theatre. She is involved in ongoing scientific research into singing at the University of Sydney and was on the development team for the unique software, Sing&See™. In addition, she is a major contributor to international publications on the subject of voice. Her book, The Singing Voice: An Owner's Manual *(Currency, 2001), is an amazing, practical, and essential guide for singers in musical theatre, jazz, pop, and rock.*

PERSPECTIVE

Will you say something about your background and about what influenced or informed your approach to teaching?

Okay, you're going to have the story of my life, but it'll be very quick. This is about me and what has informed my life as a teacher, as a musician, as a performer. I was born in a shoebox and left on the front doorstep of the Presbyterian Babies' Home in Canterbury Road, Camberwell, in Melbourne, where the good Presbyterians picked me up with the milk and the papers. And shortly thereafter, this being 1943, my birth mother appeared on the doorstep, and from her the Presbyterians found out three things: (1) She was of Dutch ethnicity; (2) she was *very* musical; and (3) she was a very bad girl, bearing in mind this was 1943 and a woman that didn't have a bloke to show for it . . . for shame, for shame! That babies' home was run along the lines of a great reformer in children's and neonate care, Truby King (Dr. Frederick Truby King), a New Zealander, and they believed passionately in nurturing whatever might have been there genetically, so they would not adopt me out unless one of the presenting adopting parents was intensely musical. So they pinned nappies on me for nine months, until I was adopted out to my parents, they whom I call *parents* because, hell, they did the parenting. My mother couldn't tell you "Pop goes the king" from "God save the weasel," but my father was a conservatorium-trained basso and just a beautiful singer. So music formed a crossroads in my life from when I was born. And when I was very young, my adoptive parents told me how I was adopted and I was not like the kids next door. They got me from a special baby shop—wasn't that neat? The kid who was selected! They also told me that my birth mother was highly musical and that I was put there because the home hoped that I would have music, too. And so my father was a wonderful singer and he was my singing teacher till I got to that teenage year when you think your parents don't know anything. I went to other singing teachers, but it was the foundation of my musicianship, my cultural basis, my performance experiences—working with this brilliant man. So that's the background that informs my music. And every time as a little kid, when my parents were cross with me, I used to think, "Oh, you went and got me, didn't you? Brought it on your own head!" So that's the flip side of adoption. Feels great. And also, you can't look at a whole pile of maiden aunts and think, "Holy shit, I'm gonna look like that in fifty years!" I haven't a clue. So that's pertinent.

*Do you work with students on classical as well as musical
theatre repertoire? Do you teach vocal styles other than classical
and/or musical theatre?*

My initial singing and piano training was in classical. My father was a
classical singer—oratorio, opera, art song. I used to do that stuff, too. My
piano training from when I was very, very young, also the same. I lost my
virginity when I was thirteen, by hearing a record of Errol Garner playing
"Concert by the Sea." That was my *musical* virginity, I mean, of course. Well,
I thought, "Oh, you can make things up. Wow!" And so, although I have all
the foundational training of classical, I now do not teach classical; I primarily teach music theatre, in which I'm very much more at home. I'm a
specialist in repertoire. I also teach people in rock and roll and jazz. I particularly like working with jazz repertoire and teaching people improvisation.
I enjoy that lots.

*I gathered that. Your book is such a fun read and I just felt,
"This is a person who has been there, who is still there,
and who really knows this from the inside out."*

Well, thank you.

*How would you describe the vocal requirements for singers in musical
theatre today? How have those requirements changed over the years
and where do you think they're going?*

Shall we start with where it was, then to where it is, and then where it's going?

Right.

Where it was, was an offshoot of classical technique. I refer to . . . what's it
called? *Black Crook*, that archetypal, ancient American music theatre piece,
about 1866, into operetta, Romberg, Herbert, Novello, which has a sort of
a dribble-on effect into Coward, in all of which you're using legit voice. You
need a sound classical training, because you cannot put a legit voice on top
of somebody that's half-trained. That's where it was in the old musicals.
You'd sing Kern like that; you'd sing Gershwin. We still debate, Is *Porgy
and Bess* an opera or not? My favorite definition concerns *Sweeney Todd:
Sweeney Todd* is an opera when the orchestra's in black tie, and *Sweeney Todd*

is a musical when the orchestra's in black T-shirts. That, to me, speaks about the boundary between classical and music theatre. Jeanette MacDonald, Kathryn Grayson, all *sound*, legit voices, with great classical base. You'd have the character pieces, and the work that the character singers would do in music theatre goes back to British music hall. "Somebody stole my gal. Somebody stole my pal" [singing]. That's the comic relief. That's the "I'm just a girl that can't say no" thing, and they, I think, go back in theatrical tradition beyond music hall, but that's a quick reference for all of us. Where it is now—I could give you a full list—in fact, I did that in the conference I've just done in New Zealand—a full list of all musical genres found in musical theatre, and it's the whole works! It is classical, it is gospel, it is rock and roll, it is pop, it is *Bring in 'Da Noise, Bring in 'Da Funk*, it's rap. It is world music, it is jazz—Cy Coleman writes jazz, for heaven's sake—*City of Angels*. Every range of music is catered for in music theatre, so you cannot be a snob. You cannot say, "Oh, I want to do music theatre but I only want to work in legit voice." Well, you can, but you're not going to make money for your agent and you're not going to make money for you, QED, you're not going to be in the business, and show business is called a *business*. So where it is now is a huge range of demands and to answer from a commercial viewpoint, it's also run by people who have intense strictures on their time and money. Therefore, if you cannot encompass the range of styles in the show for which you have auditioned, then there's a merciless commercial feeling that says, "You can't do it, you're out the door." There's no sentimentality. To me, that's where music theatre now is for its singers. A huge range of possibilities, a huge range of demands, maximum flexibility, and fairly pitiless if you can't cut it. Where it's going (the cynic in me says), because of the cost of this art form, which, much like its big sister, opera, is money intensive, labor intensive, time intensive, we will see the growth of two-handers like *The Last Five Years* and *John and Jen*; chamber musicals such as *I Love You, You're Perfect, Now Change*, and *Baby*; those ones that will take six people and a piano, bass, drums. And you can tour the buggers and it doesn't cost the earth. And I think we have seen the last of the helicopters and the chandeliers. It is my guess.

I also think our audiences now are demanding more engaging plot lines, more interesting, theatrically based experiences, rather than just gimme the spectacle, the eighty-five dancing girls. You look at *Crazy for You*, you look at *Sugar Babies*, which burlesques the burlesque, which I love, but that was spectacle of its day, too. Now I think we look at what are people watching on television? What do they watch in the movies, what are the storylines, the circumstances, and the philosophies that engage people so that the catharsis happens? I mean, you know, that's what we're here for: Have a cathart! Seventy-five bucks worth of cathart, please—that's my business, thank you. And they want reality, they want truth in their acting; they are merciless when it comes to hammy, overperforming, unless it's, say, in a satirical piece, which people really say the Americans can't do, but I think they can. You look at *The Producers*. If that's not satire, I'll eat my hat. I think where we're heading is a tremendous amount of theatrical truth, smaller shows, more pungent theatre experiences, and less of an emphasis on huge spectacles. My crystal ball.

Why do you teach what you teach? What drives you? What is your passion in this work?

I teach what I teach because *wonderful* people have given it to me, and I owe it to them to give as much as I can, as unencumbered by my values, my prejudices, my fears, or my hopes, as clearly as I can, to other people, so that they, too, may be as advantaged as I have been. There is a debt of honor here for me, and I don't just refer to my dear old dad. I have, as we all do, this line of great people on whose shoulders we are standing. In acknowledging them, I honor them, whenever I maybe get it right. So why I teach is that. The next bit of the question?

What drives you? What is your passion?

What drives me is love. To me, it's the one fuel that doesn't clog up the system. When you burn that love, there's no toxic remains. So I love what I'm doing if I *love* being in the same room with the people I'm working with, those actors, that person. If I love the material, the genre, if I don't look down my nose at it and think, "I could have been in *Madame Butterfly* if I wasn't so short." If I love and honor the genre for what it is, then that fuel keeps me going. That's what drives me.

What role does voice science, or vocal anatomy and physiology, play in your work with students or clients?

Voice science has played an increasing role in my practice. As I've learnt more—it just comes in the front door to me and I take it with the passion of the newly converted. I did a postgrad study with Jean Callaghan some few years ago on singing pedagogy. I knew a bit of stuff before that, of course, but the formalization of that knowledge in that course was so specifically for people teaching singing, and it was the science of voice, the physiology of it, the anatomy of it, and that sort of stuff immediately made huge differences. Now I'm doing voice research myself. I'm halfway through my master's looking at what singers observe when they're looking at a computer screen with their own voice on it. How do they make sense of a coded pattern that is purporting to be their voice, either in pitch or timbre? So I'm, for the first time that I can find in research, looking at how people decode while they're busy doing this magical singing thing we do.

Does movement or movement-based training play a role in your teaching?

Because I work with actors whose instruments are their whole spirit and their whole body, and because I, too, am a performer, I will always do bodywork first. In fact, I can't think of a time where I would start a class with actors, where we wouldn't have done some movement first. I think phonation comes most safely and easily out of a moved body.

Yes!

Amen?

Amen!

And rather than me grabbing you by the throat and saying, "Hey, let's squeeze some sound out of you," what's happening is that your gross muscles are allowing and endorsing the phonation in a way that's going to be the most natural and will most complement any work you'll need to do onstage in future. So all I'm doing is setting up a foundation, but when you've got to walk out there in front of people and either speak or sing, all you do is elongate the odd vowel and give the vowel a bit of pitch. It's the same job. I, as audience, either believe you or I don't. And if it doesn't come from the body, I don't *believe* you. You can sit there with the best little face in the world and say, "I really put expression into that, Pat." And I'll say, "I looked at your left knee and I didn't believe you, Honey." That body will never tell me a lie. So body first, always.

I couldn't agree more. Do you use any recording equipment in your studio? Do you teach microphone techniques?

I do have recording equipment in my home studio because I often play accompaniments for people. They all sometimes bring along mini-discs, which is a great technology, too, or MP3s, those little tiny guys, and I'll just record practice accompaniments for them to sing along to. I don't record people's voices in the studio. Here's a good reason why. When I sing into a microphone (and I've done it a lot in studios), a machine is going to record me and play back and tell me how it heard me, but no machine hears me the way a pair of human ears hears me, and if I'm working with a young, unformed performer, I can devastate them by saying, "See, Priscilla, you were flat on that second bar, weren't you dear?" And they won't hear that they were flat; they'll just hear, "It doesn't sound like *me*!" And there's nothing more depersonalizing. I don't know about linear predictive coding, or LPC, but it sounds great. It's a way of programming algorithms, so that when you acoustically grab the voice, you record it in a way that the human ear hears it. I like it! So I'd go that one.

So would I!

THE TRAINING

Where do you start? What are the vital signs you check right away when a student comes to you? What are the foundational aspects of training to which you regularly attend?

Where do I start, with somebody I've never seen before, or with somebody who is in again for their weekly visit?

Either way.

Okay. I always start with the spirit—sorry—because you can look right, you can *seem* wonderful, you can say, "Let's get going." But if I know that there's something between you and the work, we might as well just sit down and say, "How's your week been?" Not ever to invade. I am not a psychologist and don't try to be, and I have a horror of it, but if my intuition tells me you're not ready to work, my job is to make sure you work in an optimal way, and sometimes maybe we're not having a lesson today. But we're having a cup of tea. You don't have to tell me any more, but today's not a singing day. I might throw you some more repertoire, some stuff in areas you've not worked in yet, but today, Nah, give your little voice a rest. So I think I'll always start with the spirit, and also in a group, very much so in a group of actors. If a group's not in the right place, there's no point in me saying, "Right-o, shoes off. Right-o, we're going to do stretches *right now*." So, spirit first. Then body, then very light phonation and checking the posture during light phonation. "Hello, where's the neck, where's the head, where's the shoulders, are the knees softened, is there a release, is there an *allowance* of the sound, or are you just squeezing something a bit like a toothpaste tube?" I try to keep away from what I call the "singing police" side of things: "Make sure you're in pitch, that was not in rhythm, your timbral quality's wrong." I will mostly start with exercises where it doesn't matter what pitch you sing. So I will do the phonation and the phonation into singing, with extended tone, just keeping an eye on where the body is, and I'll then go into, probably, singing words. That would be my continuum.

What do you expect to observe in a singer that is well trained or in a performer who sings well, with or without training?

To observe is to hear, to see, to smell, to perceive, to intuit, all that stuff. A wonderful singer communicates instantly to me. And I'm not saying that they've got the best voice, but a wonderful singer will tell me stuff and I'll know I've been told! There's no repenting from that position. You send it to me; I got it *good*. The externals that I would notice in them would include a body that tells the same story that the neck's telling. What's coming out the neck and what the body's radiating is exactly the same. There's a coherence, an integration. I know it sounds weird, but I would notice that they wouldn't be trying to sing.

Oh, yes. Absolutely.

You know what I mean. They'd just be telling me stuff. Whether they were acting as in spoken text, or acting as a singer, I would have, I think, the same sense of being communicated with clearly and strongly and with an intensity of focus that makes me aware of the nuances they want me to get. That's what I'd notice, I think.

Great. Granted, the journey is different from one singer to another, but would you say something about how students might get from A to B, or from their first lessons with you to a solid professional technique?

It sounds like a woolly question, but it isn't. How a student would get from their very first lessons to working professionally. I see these steps. Initially, a collegiality and trust between the two of us. This would hold good either in a group of twenty-five students in a theatre training school or one on one in my studio. We don't even have to like each other, but there's a sense of trust between us. If that's not there, go home and knit socks. On the basis of that, then, a contractual understanding that if they will give time to this sport called singing, which will be solitary, consistent, physical activity, then I'm here as their sports coach to support them. If then they show an assiduousness in this, I start looking at building the actor and the spirit within there, learning based on the fact that the body's starting to build a muscular foundation (and they'll remember 'cause the muscles remember it): a technique for that performer. Then I'd see performance opportunities, which in my case are almost always auditions. I prepare people for professional auditions. I'm very good at it and I like it. That's my gig. So I don't hold studio concerts. I never send them to eisteddfodau (competitions). I find that a very negative and particularly perilous activity on occasion, where flautists and timpanists will tell vocalists how good or bad they are. It's a bit of a mug's game really. So that would be the next continuum. Ready for performance? Okay, go and impress five bored people over there with cold coffee with this little song that you've got. Make them believe that you are that person, you've got these problems, and you'd love them to help you with your problem. And from that, you do the job.

In the answers to earlier questions, you have certainly touched on some, if not all, of the six aspects of training listed below:

Alignment, Breathing, Range, Resonance, Articulation, Connection (the Acting Dimension)

Now, from the perspective of your own approach, will you comment specifically on each of these technical elements, to whatever extent and in whatever order you choose?

Okay. *Alignment.* I'm always working with bodies and I use a lot of floor work because you then get the head and the shoulders and the neck and the spine in their correct relationships with the least amount of strain, without me having to say, "Do this, push that." Suddenly the pipes open, *ahh*! And then transferring what you've learned to the ninety degrees. I'll work on walls, sliding down a wall until your quads hurt and making sure your feet are reasonably close to the wall, not way away from it. Those sorts of tricks are wonderful for assuring alignment in the body.

Breathing. When you've got people on the floor, you can see if they've got held breathing patterns, and an actor has to pick that up really, really early. I'm amazed at how many acting teachers don't spot it. It is we voice and singing teachers who have to hold that particular fort and be especially vigilant because I've known it to take three years for a particularly stubborn and held man's torso to get a free, released breathing pattern that is in harmony with what his lungs and his diaphragm want to do.

Range. The thing I'd like to say about that is I would work from the middle, what you'd call, I suppose, modal range, the talking thing, and I would work out to the upper and down to the lower and consistently both ways. And I don't care if little Mary Jane wants to get the highest note. I have a very strong picture in my head of those men that go to the gym because they want a great set of pecs, and they go in, do this wonderful muscle work. They come out half a year later with the pecs of death and this sad little butt and tiny little matchstick legs. So for me a voice has to match, and so start in the middle, build out the front, build out the back, and it all stays in balance. I find that the muscularity involved in that, building both ways, gently, at the same time, means that you get the greatest stability in the low voice. It's less likely to be frail. And you've got a more sure high voice in that, too—a solid top.

Resonance. Our fashions in theatre have changed. There was a time when your theatre voice [demonstrating rich, full-bodied, formal sound] involved that. Now, I think, these days, stylistically, the only people we've got left are the radio people that talk like this [deep, authoritative voice]. Once upon a time I used to have a radio program on the ABC, which is the posh national station [continuing to use radio voice]. And when I had my program I sounded as if I was in a diving bell. Oh, my. That's what they wanted. But now, so much theatre and music theatre is being written for regional dialect. In Britain it's not RP anymore. You've got Estuary. Jamie Oliver's your standard Estuary sound, init [in dialect]? And that's an amalgam of your Cockney, your Sussex and a bit of RP, and it's those very interesting linguistic soups happening, not just in England, but that's a good example, and stuff's being written—theatre and music theatre—for those accents and dialects. So the resonance has to encompass all sorts of stuff now. I think you also *have* to do RP, and you have to know how to go there, but these days you need to have lots and lots of tools in your toolbox or you're unemployable, vide previous comments about the range of genres in music theatre now. Hallelujah!

Articulation. In every class, whether I teach individually or in a group, I will always teach articulatory stuff, tongue twisters. And it's just something that's always accepted. It's a kind of competition. Can I do it quicker this week? And it's desperately necessary. We are losing our /l/ in Australia.

Really? Is it going to a /w/?

Yes. It's the one that's going the soonest, but /r/ is being lost, too. It is fascinating what's happening in our language. Bits of it are eliding and one of the things I frequently say to people is, "I don't teach many people to sing really, but I do teach people to hear, to listen." I teach people to be aware of their language and how much of it people are eliding out of existence. They've got to know what's in there, so articulation is to *hear* and to be aware of what you're saying. Desperately important.

Okay, *connection.* I have a little book that I've written called, *The Song Workbook.* It hasn't been published; it's just something I give to my students. And in it I demand that students analyze every song from the point of view of paraphrasing all the lyric, speaking it as a monologue, imagining a set of circumstances under which an imagined character—not the person from the show—an imagined character could . . . I would say it to them, "Where are they, what shoes have they got on their feet?" All very Stanislavski. Then I've got ten games that they can play with that lyric in order to make the best acting sense of it. Written games. Actors sometimes love 'em, sometimes hate 'em. But at least do three or four of those on every song and then you know that you have a proper actorly appreciation of the text and you know what you're talking about.

Again, from your perspective, how do these individual aspects of training relate to one another in the learning process and then in performance?

All those disparate elements are, to me, like separate tools in a toolbox that get specific jobs done. A hammer is not a chisel is not a saw, and in rehearsal and in learning, each one of them has its place where you will feature it and make a performer utterly, consciously aware. "Your articulation, Gavin. Let's just play games with your articulation today." We're both thinking about it; we're featuring it. But in performance if Gavin thinks about articulation, Honey, he's dead. If he cares about his posture, forget it; he won't get the job. If he's worried about his range, his breathing, his resonance . . . So all of those things are tools which we grab out of our tool bag, and together with our students we explore all the options that those tools can give each one of those students. And we do it consciously, with a lively sense of *play*. I don't know anything better than mucking around, play, for range, for instance.

Yes, absolutely!

But in performance, here's how it works for me, and I suppose that's all any human can say. For me, in performance, I have no technique and I don't give a rat's ass for articulation. I don't care about resonance, but I care *desperately* about those words I'm singing to you because they're mine. This is my dilemma or this is my joy. You *must* know, don't go out that door, you must hear this *now*! I think that would be the relative position. If all those things are fully embodied, then the artist can proceed to embody the text by connecting to it with honesty, and without any conscious technical concerns.

Do you have additional comments you would like to make?

You are fun!

So are you! And I'm not the least bit surprised.

You have a lovely skill at eliciting—not soliciting, thank you. You make beautiful, big spaces for people to put things in.

Well, I'm learning.

Selected Publications

Callaghan, J., & Wilson, P. 2003. *How to Sing and See: Singing Pedagogy in the Digital Era*. Sydney: Cantare Systems.

Wilson, P. 2001. *The Singing Voice: An Owner's Manual*. Sydney: Currency Press; London: Nick Hern Books.

———. 2003, "Sinful Modern Music: Science and the Contemporary Commercial Singer." *Australian Voice 9*: 12–16.

———. 2004. "The Voice and its Metaphors." *Australian Voice 10*: 16–19.

———. 2004. "On Singing Straws and Water Bottles: The Physics of Pressure." *Australian Voice 10*: 85–86.

Web site: www.patwilson.com.au

15. AMANDA COLLIVER

It was late on a Saturday afternoon and I'd not met Amanda Colliver before. Very graciously, she'd agreed to be interviewed after a day of teaching, and at the weekend. It was winter, so the light was already fading, and as I walked to the door I was not quite sure this was the place. Soon, however, Amanda greeted me warmly and invited me

Photography by Helen Madden Photographic Studio

in. The house was comfortable, done in soft colors, and large windows opened it to the rugged beauty of the trees and foliage outside. As I set the recording equipment on the coffee table in front of a large sectional sofa, Amanda's chocolate border collie joined us, and over the next hour or so I was privileged to hear the remarkable story of this gifted teacher and singer/songwriter.

Amanda Colliver began teaching twenty-five years ago and became one of the most sought-after and respected teachers in Australia. She has acted as vocal advisor to many professional productions, including Phantom of the Opera, Les Misérables, Showboat, Boy from Oz, *and* Beauty and the Beast, *and she has been a vocal tutor at the National Institute of Dramatic Arts (NIDA), in Sydney. Amanda's private practice has included preparing Hugh Jackman for his roles in* Beauty and the Beast *and* Sunset Boulevard, *Nicole Kidman and Ewan McGregor for* Moulin Rouge, *and Miranda Otto for* The Lord of the Rings. *She regularly works with recording artists, actors, dancers, songwriters, and movement specialists; and speech pathologists frequently refer postoperative patients to her for vocal rehabilitation. She is now on the faculty of the LaSalle–SIA College of the Arts, in Singapore.*

PERSPECTIVE

Where and whom do you teach? Who are your students or clients?

I teach at home so that I can set up an environment that's conducive to feeling safe. The door is always open, so students just come in and make themselves at home. My clients are generally reasonably high-profile professional singers, but I listen to everyone who wants me to. Sometimes there are people who aren't singing professionally but have excellent voices. I tend not to teach singers under the age of sixteen, as I prefer dysfunctional adults like myself.

Yes, I can relate to that. Will you say something about your background and about what influenced or informed your approach to teaching?

My background was almost entirely classical. Both my parents were choristers and strictly religious. This meant that contemporary music was not permitted in our home, with the exception of Nana Mouscouri and other very light ambiences. Although I was songwriting and in a band, my *sound* was already showing signs of classical leaning. I did a lot of amateur theatre first, Gilbert and Sullivan and some lighter musical theatre shows, and then joined the Victoria State Opera Company.

Within four years I was understudying and then moved on to become a soloist with all the other major opera companies in Australia. Twenty-three years later I walked away from my operatic career and began exploring a more contemporary approach. In essence, I began to sing the way I was teaching. So the interesting thing is that I specialized in opera, and yet have worked primarily with contemporary singers. Strangely, I've always known how to teach it, but hadn't ever done it myself.

Subsequently, I've spent the last three years exploring the styles I wasn't exposed to as a child and an amazing thing happened along the way. The old wives tales re chest voice singing proved to be wrong, and what happened was opposite to the educational information I was used to hearing. In classical singing, the chest voice is virtually surgically removed and made irrelevant to the development of the voice. A very unhealthy belief that this register will damage one's voice is instilled, and it is not only classical singers who hold this fear. Only the incorrect use of any register can and will result in damage, and I'd say that this would lie in the teaching, wouldn't you?

Personally, by using the chest register, not only have I gained a tone at the top of my classical voice, but the usually weak middle register is stronger. I believe that this is because the contemporary use of the voice strengthens the *grounding* aspect, which, in turn, impacts on the entire voice.

What I really want to do is what my students do, and part of my exploration is on a muscular level. Classical production requires a different muscular demand to chest voice, and after using head voice only for all those years, there is an imbalance between the registers for me. What I'm also saying is, "Look, I'm sorry, but I don't believe much of anything that is being said. I'm doing it and I'm proving that much of our understanding of the human instrument is limited." So that's my background, primarily classical, operatic singing.

Do you work with students on classical as well as musical theatre repertoire? Do you teach vocal styles other than classical and/or musical theatre?

I tend not to teach opera singers, although I have worked with some on their technique. Opera asks for great pianistic skills and extensive knowledge in both styles and languages. It's more about perfection and precision and is a very specific art form. My interest in it was the incredible discipline it took and the huge satisfaction in achieving it. I became very much in demand as a teacher when *Phantom of the Opera* hit the theatres and music theatre performers needed the extra skill of classical singing without sounding too operatic. Having the operatic skill and also experience as a contemporary singer was the perfect combination needed for this show. These singers are people who haven't done much in the way of making classical shapes or sounds, so I became incredibly interested in "restumping the house," so to speak. I have always taught a classical base; it demands the most of the body, the most of the instrument. There is nothing more demanding, so we start with the most difficult and peel back from there. Then it's easy to allow a style to modify what they're doing and there's no danger of sounding operatic. I think you have to work very hard to sing a pop song like an opera singer. You just wouldn't. Well, some opera singers do because they don't know how to drop the style. They don't know how to take off the "hat" because they identify with the hat.

When I introduce students to operatic shapes and sounds, they are all self-conscious about sounding "fake." I then say, "It *is* fake." There's no other vocal style more produced than this one, and those of us who earned a living from it learned how to adopt this posture. This allows them to get their heads around producing sounds they wouldn't ordinarily be making. I've worked with a number of singers with vocal fatigue, polyps, or nodules, and this has been very, very interesting for me as I don't work from a physiological point of view. Each time we have resolved it together through placement, through the realignment of the vibration with the use of classical singing. One particular recording artist, who had regularly been losing his voice, asked me for help but said in the same breath, "I don't want to sound like Denis Walter" (Denis Walter being a very good middle-of-the-road singer but with a classical sound). I still insisted that he undergo classical exercises but promised him he would only sound like a better version of himself.

One day after a recording session he said, "Ah, this is fantastic! I don't lose my voice anymore and the only difference is the clarity, the quality, with no vocal strain."

How would you describe the vocal requirements for singers in musical theatre today? How have those requirements changed over the years and where do you think they're going?

I must admit that I don't see the requirements being mapped out for anyone, except in institutions specifically geared toward music theatre performers. Generally, singers tend to go to auditions hoping they will suit the genre of the piece they are auditioning for. Many don't seem to know much about the differing styles or have the repertoire to support it. Across the board, over twenty-four years of teaching, the area I cover the most is clarifying the differences between the genres. Generally, their technique is an eclectic mix of pop, classical, and music theatre, all rolled into one, which is why they encounter problems when asked to sing one or the other. I don't mean to suggest in any way that these singers are not highly talented; in fact, they simply haven't clarified the foundational technique before becoming vocally creative. So I clean that up, helping them understand that classical demands this, rock and pop asks for communication rather than perfection, and something in between is required for musical theatre. That being said, I don't generally find an understanding of requirements by singers in Australia.

In answer to "Have the requirements changed?" I would say very much so. There used to be a time when one could more easily fly by the seat of one's pants, but not any more. Instead of the three components of singing, dancing, and acting being separated, the requirement now is that you can do all three equally as well, and there are those who can. The benchmark is higher now, so people are wanting to know more, do more, be more.

Why do you teach what you teach? What drives you? What is your passion in this work?

My passion, in one word, is healing. The healing of myself, the healing of others, and the obliteration of the fears that prevent us all being the magnificent creative beings that we are. Although I have sung since I was a child, stage fright haunted me for years, turning something that I loved and could not live without, into something to be feared. My own struggle has left me not only with an empathy for all other performers, but with an absolute understanding of how psychologically driven the act of singing is. Although it is a physical act, the mind affects the body. Subsequently, no amount of mechanistic control will override the sabotage of fear. Fear, I believe, has everything to do with the need for approval. Nothing more, nothing less. A lack of validation in my earlier years impacted on my confidence in my own abilities. Generally, I think we all struggle with this one in one degree or another, although, that being said, I have worked with a handful of people who are completely comfortable in their own skin and are only in need of more technical information.

I am greatly inspired by the intuitive side of teaching and, apart from being a trained technician, somehow I can see blockage within a singer's body and I can hear the "soul sound" that sits within the body before they even know they can make it. I love the challenge of changing my language to make a concept understood and I love inspiring people to look for their own answers. All these things are what drives me to teach.

What role does voice science, or vocal anatomy and physiology, play in your work with students or clients?

You're gonna love this—absolutely none. But I tried. I really tried to learn about the anatomy of the voice but something kept pulling me back to the organic feeling of the voice, not the technical analysis of it.

And your father's a speech pathologist.

That's right, but it plays no part in my teaching, inasmuch as I digest, but I don't consciously digest for myself. I sing, but I don't consciously manipulate my vocal cord.

I believe that these things should manipulate themselves and that the conscious mind does not know how this is done. I see people lifting, pushing, helping, and I don't disagree that a certain result should be happening, but my premise is that the perfect action is always trying to happen. I hear teachers saying, "You need height, you need height." I prefer to say, "Why isn't height happening?" Or, "You need more support," and I prefer to say, "Why isn't your support working?" If I can get singers to stop doing things, the body will show them just how much it does on its own. Occasionally, I will address the cricoid cartilage in relationship to registers, but I teach people to recognize the sensations of the voice from within.

Does movement or movement-based training play a role in your teaching?

Yoga does and the little work I did in Alexander does. Yoga makes one aware of the importance of the stability of the breath and the grounding or earthing of the body. The body, being the singer's instrument, must be centered in a way that keeps it stable and free. An awareness of the way we take air into the body impacts completely on the results we achieve when engaging sound. The awareness that sound is anchored in the pelvis, or base chakra, impacts enormously on the quality and control of the voice. Yoga is very much about the *inner eye* . . . meditation, concentration, and manipulation. It requires that you feel bodily movement internally rather than externally or conceptually.

Alexander Technique, as I experienced it, showed me the importance of introducing a physical action to achieve a vocal result. For example, if students are having difficulty with the legato line within a phrase, I might get them to sing the phrase and pretend they are painting a wall. If the body is engaged in a sweeping action, it is quite hard not to do the same thing with your voice. Also, working in opposites is very helpful. For example, if I think down when attempting a high note, I am more likely not to disconnect my sound and if I think up as I descend, I'm far less likely to collapse. There are all sorts of ways of autosuggesting an equilibrium within the body.

Do you use recording equipment in your studio? Do you teach microphone techniques?

No, not really. However, I would love to begin to video people while they sing, as so much can be seen on the face in relationship to the sound working or not. The most common fault is the lack of communicative expression. Because concentration is present, it is easy to deaden the animation aspect of communicating. Even when a scale is being sung, it is still the communication of music and will eventually exist in the singing of words in the context of a song. Singing is an extension of speech, but it is easy to forget this whilst undergoing technical training.

THE TRAINING

Where do you start? What are the vital signs you check right away when a student comes to you? What are the foundational aspects of training to which you regularly attend?

Rather than take someone through scales, I ask them to sing me something from their repertoire. It's not an audition, but I find when people sing a song it's not only easier, but a little more of their personality tends to come through. If they don't have any repertoire, I pull out something they will know and play it in a few different keys just to hear what they're doing, or I might take people through a contemporary piece and then ask them to show me something more classical. This is to me what an x-ray is to a doctor. I suppose the vital signs are pitch, rhythm, and the presence or lack of vocal trauma. I will then take them up through their range using a scale, and then I feel informed enough to jump on in.

And do whatever you see to do?

Whatever I see to do. I know immediately if there is trauma in the throat. This trauma can be from emotional issues, wrong vocal use, or both. The work I do with these people addresses more areas than perhaps someone who holds no trauma at all and with whom I can go straight into explaining and educating. By the first half-hour, I like to have validated everything they already know and how much of their voice is already doing the correct technical things. The second half-hour is to introduce them to sounds they perhaps haven't made before to show them other possibilities and options. The foundational aspects I always attend to are based on what I perceive about the individual. Obviously, the areas we've discussed in the Perspective section are always attended to, but I'm more interested in how individuals "tick," how they think, what language they relate to, whether they are lateral thinkers, how to help them trust the process, and so forth. Until this is addressed, technical work is not as effective.

What do you expect to observe in a singer who is well trained or in a performer who sings well, with or without training?

There is an ease within the body and a sense that they and their voices are one. Range, pitch, and the use of vocal color are all the ingredients of a fine singer. The courage to break rules and an understanding of the requirements to cross over into other genres is a must.

Granted, the journey is different from one singer to the another, but would you cite a couple of examples of how students might get from A to B, or from their first lessons with you to a solid professional technique?

Well, I don't think it's possible to get a solid technique without the foundational discipline. There's repetition and muscular work that simply has to be done. One can make wonderful sounds, but the sustaining of them, the stamina aspect, is a process and that will always take time. There's a commitment, an absolute commitment, and I've not seen anyone who did not have it go anyplace very far. But those I've seen push through and actually trust the process have achieved amazing results. The other essential aspect is what I call the "fire in one's belly," the desire to do it. That having been said, I believe that balance is the key. To become a great technician does not necessarily mean to become a great performer. Regimented practice rituals lead to a noncreative mind, and although I agree that a solid technical structure must be in place at all times, there is an element of nurture sadly lacking in most performers' approach. To gain the most out of the human instrument, a singer must understand that it will not respond exactly the same way every moment of the day. Many things influence the voice and, although a general consistency must be expected, the conditions on the day must be considered. This, I believe, is part of a good technique. Tune in to how you feel, go gently while warming up, change the combinations of exercises, or simply have a day off. Most of all, from looking back at my own journey, I don't see enough support for singers' intuition; what's right for them to sing and how their voice wants to sing it. I encourage students to ask questions when they don't understand something. Ask a teacher to back up their information and be careful of being so eager to please that you ignore your body's warning signals.

To be a well-rounded performer, a great deal of listening must be done. Listening not only from an historical point of view, but from an inspirational angle. We are all influenced by others—not to become someone else, but to see and hear how they do things, their "isms" and their ways of communicating. So, in summary, play, make them your own, and then lay them all on a solid foundation of technique.

In the answers to earlier questions, you have certainly touched on some, if not all, of the six aspects of training listed below:

Alignment, Breathing, Range, Resonance, Articulation, Connection (the Acting Dimension).

These are the basic building blocks of theatre voice, and I'd like to know what you might say about these elements in your own teaching.

The science of *alignment* is that when things are aligned, all coordinations are possible. *Breathing, range, resonance, articulation,* and *connection* are all by-products of this. I believe alignment of the human voice is centered within the "energized-released" posture of the body. Stability and balance from the feet up is essential, with no extraneous work going on from the neck or jaw. Sound, however, is anchored in the perineum, and strength and awareness within the pelvic floor are paramount.

Any thoughts on breathing?

I tend not to teach breathing, but I do bring the students' awareness to how they breathe and the repercussions vocally of not breathing correctly. I believe that correct breathing is a natural function that can only be interrupted by stress. Helping people address or recognize how a particular form of stress within their body is impacting on their breath, which, in turn, impacts on their sound, helps them to begin to breathe naturally. By removing symptoms, we access the natural process.

This, I suppose, addresses the psychological aspect, the number one player. People believe that lots of air equals lots of sound. Actually, the opposite is true. By teaching them that tonal quality is in essence created by an absence of air, their approach to engaging the onset of the breath begins to change. The fear of running out is lessened and a tuning in to what is needed for any particular phrase begins to develop. When fear is present, air becomes high. I help students understand that this symptom is not something they need to resign themselves to. All confronting situations create fear within the body, which, in turn, creates an adverse reaction on the breath. This is then converted to a less than satisfactory sound. In the very next breath I take, I can reset it and rescue my audition, performance, or practice.

What a wonderful perspective!

Now *range*—that's an interesting one. There is a general misconception that a voice type—for example, baritone, tenor, soprano, mezzo, and contralto—denotes range. This is entirely untrue, as voice types are referring to vocal color and not range. The general thinking is that baritones can't sing as high as tenors or that mezzos can't sing as high as sopranos. This is rubbish and sets in motion an incredible amount of limited thinking. I have worked with lower voice types that have just as much ease and range as the higher voice types, and it needs to be understood that even though this range is not always accessed, the potential is always there. Every male holds the ability to access a top C and all women have the ability to scream, giving them the potential to access top Ds to top Gs. I'm not suggesting the ease with which one uses these does not differ from voice to voice, but the scientific fact is that we all have these resonances within our bodies unless born with a defect in the instrument. If anything, humans have become so judgmental of themselves and others that we're not prepared to make sounds that are ghastly. Well, I don't believe it's possible to make a wonderful sound without first uttering one that is inferior. No one goes to the gym and looks defined and muscular without first being undefined and un-muscular. Everyone begins any new venture with trepidation and awkwardness, but by making mistakes or sounding less than perfect, they will find the way. If this were not true, I would not spend another minute of my life teaching.

In other words, as long as you're not hurting yourself while you're making the sounds, you're getting somewhere.

That's right. There is an element of coming home from the gym stiff, but it doesn't mean you've damaged yourself. There is an element of fatigue that is necessary, absolutely necessary, but it's the recovery rate we look at. You don't want to strain your voice, which is a whole other thing, but if you're just a little bit worked, good.

Resonance. The fascinating thing about resonance is that you can sing two notes diametrically opposed quality-wise and still be on the same pitch. This is created by the right connection, or lack thereof, which takes us back to the beginning, which was alignment. The best way to help students to remain aligned, or connected, is to change their perception of intervals. Humans are conditioned visually and our usual point of reference vocally, is what we see written on the stave or what we see on the keyboard. These structures are simply for playing or reading purposes and have no truth in relationship to the real distance between vibrations. I couldn't tell you how sound really looks or the real distance between notes, but I can say that a vocal cord changes minutely with each interval. Disconnection is the primary symptom of buying into distance, so I help students to sing the intervals as though they were much smaller; for example, an octave jump as a third or even as a semitone. This, in turn, keeps the voice connected and the resonance intact. I believe there is what I call an X factor to resonance, and that is intention. Emotion colors sound, which is created through imagination, which is based on understanding. When there is an emotional intention present, sound quality changes. I don't believe this can be manipulated technically but it, in itself, manipulates technique.

Articulation. I believe if nothing is preventing the placement of the voice, you will have articulation. Primarily I find people doing too much with the mouth in an effort to articulate.

Are you saying that they're articulating in the wrong way, for example, substituting the jaw and overusing facial muscles?

Yes. I use the ventriloquism analogy a lot. This proves that sound does not rely on the mouth moving or being open. In acting Shakespeare or something un-miked, there is a whole technique to articulation, much like opera, but you just don't need it in contemporary singing. In fact, I have to get a lot of contemporary singers to under articulate because their singing is just so "straight."

What about musical theatre? Is that in between?

Well, it is certainly less articulated than classical or operatic singing.

It depends on the style, doesn't it?

Yes, it does depend on the style, but there is no style as extreme as opera sung in English.

However, I often find that opera sung in English is difficult to understand because singers don't use the consonants.

You know, I just think if you can't understand the words, then the placement is being compromised, what I call *covering the voice*. This is not what I consider to be good technique, and there are those who sing with great beauty of tone and articulation.

True . . . The acting dimension?

No performance is truly moving or complete without the connection to text. I will often ask students to speak the lyric over the music to gain a more spoken understanding than a sung one. It's easy to get caught up in making beautiful sounds rather than in what is being said. Neither one should compromise the other, and when the components of both music and text come together, we have something greater than either one on its own. This would have to be the greatest challenge for a performer.

Again, from your perspective, how do these individual aspects of training relate to one another in the learning process and in performance?

I believe all these components make up the whole and although we can take them out of context, none will function completely on its own.

Do you have any other comments you'd like to make?

I would like to say that throughout the learning process, integration and progress come in cycles, much like growing up. There will be times when there are changes and times when one hits a plateau. Try not to worry when things are not changing as rapidly as you think they should. Everyone grows at different rates and many changes are subtle but profound. I have met singers I call "teacher junkies," who, the minute their voices are not responding as quickly as they think it should, are onto the next teacher looking for more changes more quickly. Sometimes I would recommend that singers stop learning for a few months if feeling stale, and see how well they function on their own. In the end, you are on your own anyway, so don't be afraid to take time out. The learning process is exactly that—learning—and although it never ends, everyone has the potential to be at one with their voice.

16. Liz Pascoe

*In May of 2002, I spent two glo-
rious weeks at Western Australian
Academy of Performing Arts
(WAAPA), in Mt. Lawley, WA,
near Perth. In addition to working on* Pajama Game, *I had the
privilege of teaching theatre voice
to all three years of performance
majors in acting, musical theatre,
and broadcasting. It was a
remarkable experience!*

Photography by Robin Pascoe, Stage Page

Western Australian Academy of Performing Arts is the premier training
program for musical theatre in Australia and is invariably linked to the professional scene in any discussion of musical theatre performance. On a visit to
Sydney in 2004, I attended the opening of South Pacific, where a former student from WAAPA was making her Sydney debut. As I glanced at the program
and the credits, I could hardly believe my eyes. At least nine other students
I'd known at WAAPA were also in that cast! And so it goes.

Liz Pascoe is well known to theatre voice teachers throughout Australia. She
has been at WAAPA since 1990 and is highly regarded for her work with
young, gifted actors headed for professional careers in musical theatre. Liz was
away from WAAPA at the time I was teaching there, but we met at a conference
in Sydney, and she was gracious enough to respond to my questions via e-mail and
phone conversations.

PERSPECTIVE

*Would you say something about your background and about what
influenced or informed your approach to teaching?*

I trained first as a classical pianist. At age eighteen, I started classical
singing lessons with Lucie Howell, then regarded as one of Perth's leading teachers. Miss Howell was unusual for her time in that her interest
in teaching singing took her to the Faculty of Science at the University
of Western Australia to learn some of the science of voice and sound production. I guess that from my first lessons I was in an environment of
exploring the voice as an instrument. Miss Howell retired when I was in
my second year of lessons—she was eighty-four! I then spent a few years
with Evelyn Thompson, who had been Lucie Howell's accompanist, and
then with Molly McGurk, who became my lifelong teacher, mentor,
and friend. Molly was a Churchill Fellow and had studied in London
with Lucie Manen and Paul Hamburger as well as Eric Vietheer. She
was my first introduction to bel canto.

In the early seventies I was training to be a secondary school English
and music teacher, with minors in French and German. In 1974, the
second International Society for Music Education (ISME) conference was
held in Perth, and the Austrian singer and teacher Lucie Manen gave
lectures and master classes in bel canto—her understanding of it. I took
part in these. Around this time Eric Vietheer did an Australian tour
of master classes and again I was fortunate to participate. I was studying and singing exclusively in classical style at this time, reaching
licentiate diploma level with the AMEB [Australian Music Examination
Board].

Nineteen seventy-five signaled my first school teaching appointment
[Merredin], in the Western Australian wheat belt, 3½ hours' drive from
Perth and all my music connections! But in Merredin there was a repertory
club, and very soon I was involved in plays, dinner shows, and a whole
singing and piano style hitherto unknown to me and very addictive! It was
in Merredin that I did my first work as a musical director, both for the
high school musicals and for the repertory club. It was here that I met my
husband who was (and is) a teacher of drama and literature, as well as a
writer. Pretty soon I was cowriting musicals with him for production with
the kids that we taught.

On returning to the city we continued our work with youth theatre, becoming involved with the Western Australian Youth Theatre Company and writing two major musicals for performance in Festivals of Perth in the mid-eighties. In 1988 we took thirty young actors to the Thespian Festival in Muncie, Indiana, where we performed two original music theatre pieces. Through this time we were also managing a community theatre company, which performed both straight plays and theatre restaurant shows.

In 1987, I took on my first singing students, mainly at the encouragement of Molly McGurk. These students were mainly young classical singers. In 1990, I was invited to teach at WAAPA in the Music Theatre Department. At this time, I was studying for, and gained, the T Mus A [Teacher of Music in Australia] diploma in singing voice (AMEB). Part of the research for this exam involved a study of teachers and voice scientists, such as William Vennard, Meribeth Bunch, and Richard Miller. At this stage my teaching was still heavily influenced by my own classical technique; however, I was developing an awareness of having to adjust the technique to manage different performing styles and situations. I became, and remain, fascinated by the position of the Italian vowels (and their popular/contemporary diphthong counterparts) and the use and balancing of resonances in producing an appropriate sound.

In the past ten years I have also been influenced by master classes and workshops given by Marvin Keenze, Elisabeth Howard, Helen Tiller, Irene Bartlett, yourself, and, most recently, Neil Semer, whom I found fascinating because of his connection to bel canto.

Do you work with students on classical as well as musical theatre repertoire? Do you teach vocal styles other than classical and/or musical theatre?

Most of my WAAPA music theatre students study some classical repertoire and I work on Vaccai with many of them. The time constraints of the course and ever-diminishing teaching weeks limit this. I have a little experience of teaching soft pop. In the last six months I have been having jazz voice lessons, more as a personal development project than any plan to teach it. The lessons have, however, enhanced my understanding of jazz styles and techniques.

How would you describe the vocal requirements for singers in musical theatre today? How have those requirements changed over the years and where do you think they're going?

I believe the biggest challenge for the music theatre singer today is the development and maintenance of a technique that will survive eight shows a week. Increasingly, music theatre singers need to cross over into popular/contemporary styles. It is necessary to have both a classical technique and a popular/contemporary technique these days. Recent experience with students auditioning for the Australian productions of *Mamma Mia* and *We Will Rock You* highlighted the need for music theatre singers to have a high belt technique and for teachers to be able to help them access this sound safely. Music theatre singers need to be actors and dancers, too, and, in the case of song and dance, must cope with the conflicting demands placed on the abdominal muscles.

Why do you teach what you teach? What drives you? What is your passion in this work?

I love the theatre. I love working with actors and words. There is a huge satisfaction in hearing a student develop a better sound or a more flexible technique. I also love the unique nature of every voice. I enjoy the diagnostic nature of the work. This work is never predictable!

What role does voice science, or vocal anatomy and physiology, play in your work?

I think that when I started teaching I worked mostly through imagery. As my knowledge of vocal anatomy grew, I used it to inform my teaching practice. I feel that I still have much to learn; however, I have a good understanding of body alignment, breathing, and resonance and use a combination of physiology and imagery to teach these concepts.

Does movement or movement-based training (e.g., the Alexander Technique, Feldenkrais, Pilates, or yoga) play a role in your teaching?

At WAAPA the students have Feldenkrais training. In past years Alexander Technique was also taught but has suffered from budget constraints. Just yesterday a student looked at one of the Alexander tables and asked what it was! I have taken part in short courses in both Alexander and Feldenkrais and have an awareness of these, rather than skills. My concept of alignment is based on Alexander and I have occasionally used the Feldenkrais jaw exercises.

Do you use any recording equipment in your studio? Do you teach microphone techniques?

My students record their lessons on their own personal variety of equipment, ranging from mini-disc to Dictaphone. I occasionally record them on mini-DV. I teach only the most basic of microphone techniques. The music theatre students at WAAPA, unfortunately, have very little training in microphone technique.

Are the shows miked?

Yes, body mikes are used for the WAAPA musicals, which are performed in the main theatre, but mikes are generally not used in the smaller spaces.

THE TRAINING

Where do you start? What are the vital signs you check right away when a student comes to you? What are the foundational aspects of training to which you regularly attend?

I always start by hearing a new student perform a song. I am listening to vibrancy of tone, accuracy of pitch, clarity of diction, ease of breathing, sense of phrasing, ease of moving through registers, the presence of both head and chest resonance across the range, and connection with the text. I am watching alignment, looking for tensions in the jaw, knees, and the rest of the body. I try to identify idiosyncrasies, both desirable and undesirable.

Once training begins, I regularly attend to warm-ups, alignment, breathing and resonance with all students. I work on evenness of tone throughout the range and a balance of upper and lower resonance, which inevitably leads to an increase in range. I also spend time on "reading the music," that is, discovering the intentions of the composer and lyricist and how this can inform the performance.

What do you expect to observe in a singer who is well trained
or in a performer who sings well, with or without training?

I expect to hear a freedom, flexibility, and ease and balance of tone, and not to notice *technique*. I expect to hear clarity of diction and a connection to the textual journey of the song. I expect the singer to move comfortably on stage. I expect to hear tone that supports the characterization. I expect that the singer will establish a mutual relationship with the audience, as well as with other singers/actors on stage.

Granted, the journey is different from one singer to another, but if
you think it appropriate, would you cite an example or two of how
students might get from A to B, or from their first lessons with you
to a solid professional technique?

If a student has had previous lessons (as is often the case with WAAPA students), I spend time gathering an understanding of the journey with the previous teacher. I strongly believe in working from the known to the unknown. Very often students arrive at WAAPA with a strong sense of being "belters" or "classical singers." I like to work outwards from their comfort zone with the goal of making them more technically versatile.

I work with the student in establishing a daily warm-up routine. I work with an appropriate variety of repertoire from the start, and performance practice forms an important part of the training. As the foundations of technique become established, I try to broaden the repertoire, and I am constantly working with the student to build physical and vocal stamina. New and more complex repertoire drives the development of technique. In second and third year, music theatre students are involved with productions and this gives them an opportunity to measure the success of their technique so far. The singing lesson sometimes becomes a troubleshooting session at this time. When our WAAPA students graduate, I certainly feel that they nearly always have a stronger technique than at the point of entry to the course; however, I do believe that they are often (either due to age or circumstance) still a way off a solid professional technique. I encourage them to continue their singing training after graduation.

In the answers to earlier questions, you have certainly touched on some, if not all, of the six aspects of training listed below?

Alignment, Breathing, Range, Resonance, Articulation, Connection (the Acting Dimension)

Now, from the perspective of your own approach, would you comment specifically on each of these technical elements, to whatever extent and in whatever order you choose?

Alignment is probably the fundamental in my approach to the teaching of singing. When the body is in balance, all other technical aspects tend to fall into place and the sound improves noticeably. The challenge, of course, lies in modifying alignment to meet the director's demands on stage.

Breathing. I work from a sense of release on the intake and gentle but continuous support throughout phonation. I like the concept of 360-degree support with a low abdominal/pelvic floor basis. I use exercises to make the student aware of the back ribs and muscles. Ultimately, I hope that students will find the point(s) of focus for support that best suits their own mechanism. I do quite a bit of preparatory work in semisupine.

Range. I find that I don't consciously work on range unless the range is so limited that it is necessary to do so from the start. Rather, I work on smoothing out the passaggio and on developing a balance of resonances, and that, in itself, leads to an increase in range. I am very conscious of consistency of tone throughout the range, whether in classical or popular/contemporary style.

Resonance. I spend much time on this in the early stages of training in the form of humming and placing the hands on various parts of the skull, face, and torso to sense the vibration. From this humming position I introduce the vowels, both classical (Italian) and popular/contemporary. This involves an awareness and use of the hard and soft palates. I encourage resonance exercises as part of the daily warm-up throughout the training period and beyond. I am looking to open up a balanced "spectrum" of resonance, which the singer can then access according to need; for example, the high forward resonance for pop sound or the same, plus upper head resonance and soft palate space, for a high classical sound.

Articulation. We incorporate tongue and lip exercises in warm-ups and I constantly vary the start consonant in technical exercises. In the study of

songs, articulation becomes more complex; for example, how an end consonant can initiate portamento, how the definition of consonants can
inform character choices, and so on.

Connection. The most interesting part! I like to lift the text off the music
and have the singer work with it as a monologue. Then we look at the relationship of the musical text with the word text. Which is more important
in this particular song? Or are they of equal importance? What sound
quality does the text demand? What is the journey for the singer/character?
How can his or her technique support this journey? What are the staging
or blocking needs of the song?

*Again, from your perspective, how do these individual aspects
of training relate to one another (1) in the learning process
and (2) in performance?*

This is a hard question! They are all interrelated in the learning process;
it's just that from time to time one takes greater attention than another.
In performance they are again interrelated but should be invisible and
inaudible—the audience doesn't want to see or hear a singer working on
technique. Singers need to have a solid foundation, but even when only
partly along the way, must trust whatever technique exists to work for
them in performance.

*Yes! You put it so succinctly. Do you have additional comments you
would like to make?*

This has been an interesting process. Good luck with the book! And thanks
for including me.

REFERENCE

Web site: www.stagepage.com.au

PART IV

Observations

and

Conclusions

17. Cultural Perspectives

All of the interviewees were gracious with their time and generous with the information they were willing to share. The large majority expressed (1) a keen interest in the relationship of singing to theatre voice and actor training; (2) openness to the thinking of others; and (3) an unquestionable passion for their work.

Theatre itself differs logistically from one country to another, and for a while the Australian model evaded me. Then Liz Pascoe (chapter 16) put it this way: "In the US you go to New York, in the UK you go to London, and in Australia the shows come to us." Casting is done in Melbourne and Sydney, and young actors starting out in a career usually live in one of those cities.

In New York or London, you can easily see theatre six nights a week and take in two shows a day on Tuesday, Wednesday, Thursday, and Saturday for a two-week theatre holiday. Everything is either within walking distance (New York) or easily accessible by tube (London), and well mapped out in brochures—far better in London than in New York. In Australia, however, things are much less centralized, and you should be prepared to hop a plane every few days in order to see a comparable number of shows. Fortunately, each major city has its own wonderful flavor and the theatre standard throughout the country is high.

In all three parts of the world, new works are being nurtured and produced, and distinctly Australian musicals are of particular interest in this regard. Debbie Phyland (chapter 12) notes:

∞

The Australian image is still emerging in musical theatre . . . we're getting more and more comfortable with the Australian sound, and . . . more receptive to Australian stories being told in musical format.

∞

From my own observations, Australian singers seem freer to use a legit sound a greater percentage of the time, even for contemporary material, than either their US or UK counterparts.

The ability to sing in distinctly different vocal qualities across the range of musical theatre styles is now essential to getting work in most parts of the world. Performers may be singing in a rock musical at night and rehearsing an entirely different kind of show in the daytime, or vice versa. Contractual agreements in Britain frequently make it necessary for singers to overlap the end of one show with rehearsals for another in order to keep working. Also in Britain, pop/rock is in (Meylan 2004) and musical theatre is considered more an entertainment form than an art form. In Australia, cabaret is a major trend at present, due in part to venue costs and insurance rates, which are often prohibitive for full-scale musical productions. The small population of the country is also a contributing factor to the relatively brief list of musicals on offer at any time. In the United States, variety and change are the norm, and vocal requirements of productions range from legit to gospel to country, pop, rock, and jazz.

Voice and Speech

Cultural perspectives frequently relate directly to voice and speech, and more particularly to accents and dialects. Lisa Ryan-McLaughlin (chapter 10) says, "If you watch an American movie and then watch how we speak in an Australian movie, you're going to see great physical differences with the jaw, the tongue, and the mouth, and that's what accents are about," physical differences.

Finding the appropriate voice quality for a role is invariably influenced by one's own habitual speech. Mary Saunders-Barton (chapter 5) works brilliantly with American students and teachers who have not experienced the physicality of a "brassy, sassy" Broadway sound (Debbie Phyland's evocative phrase), when she has them speak a phrase and then sing it in the same position kinesthetically, and in the same pitch range. So if the musical phrase is high, the speech is high, and vice versa. The physical sensations of a very forward placement and a fairly assertive manner are so familiar to most Americans that speech serves as a direct route to the desired quality. However, if the same exercise were used with British or

Australian singers, they would need to go through an additional step in the process, because the habitual shape of their vocal tract does not lend itself to a brassy, sassy sound.

Debbie Phyland (chapter 12) elaborates on this issue in her discussion of present-day vocal requirements for singers in musical theatre. She says, ". . . we are regularly called upon to create the Broadway sound . . . Australian singers traditionally weren't good at that because they were not used to having that really focused 'nyaaa.' We tend to produce a lazier, broader sound."

Even a single word or phrase may be culturally identifiable. So, in addition to being able to cross styles, singers in musical theatre need to take into consideration the origin of the material and its cultural perspective. Accents and dialects are often a pivotal aspect of the actor's preparation; getting a handle on the speech can be a real shortcut to the character itself in terms of physicality, voice quality, and even integral relationships. A different way of speaking equals a different person, a different set of circumstances, and infinitely different possibilities! Imagine, for example, Tony from *West Side Story* speaking Standard British, or Henry Higgins doing a New York, Mary Poppins hailing from Chicago, or Marion Woolnough (*Boy from Oz*) from Charleston, and suddenly you have four very different stories!

Although the formation of specific, differentiated vowels is regularly given considerable attention, the production and relative strength of consonants is often overlooked as an identifying factor in accents and dialects. For example, strong medial consonants just don't occur in most present-day American speech. So when actors do lovely crisp /t/ sounds in the middle of words, we know they're either not American or they're Americans trying hard to pronounce "correctly." On the other hand, when Americans do British or Australian dialects, the habit of reducing or softening consonants tends to give them away.

Likewise, /r/ sounds are made differently from one part of the world to another. So in order for British and Australian actors to sound American, they must learn to bunch the tongue toward the center of the mouth, especially for the vocalic /r/ that ends many American diphthongs, for example, in words like *heart, car, Orlando, there, ear, your*, and *actor*. Americans, on the other hand, must learn to use the tip of the tongue for the consonant /r/ in British and Australian speech.

CLASSIFICATIONS AND LABELS

Americans are fond of separating, classifying, and labeling, as in acting programs that are Meisner-based, or Stanislavski-based, and theatre voice programs that are Linklater-, Lessac-, or Fitzmaurice-based, so I fully expected to find more of a tendency to categorize among the American teachers than among teachers from the UK or Australia. To some extent that was the case. However, the labeling tendency seems fairly universal and frequently serves as an efficient way of distinguishing among contrasting approaches. For example, Gillyanne Kayes' Vocal Process relates directly to her expressed concern for "*what* makes the voice work" (chapter 9), Jeannette LoVetri's Contemporary Commercial Music (CCM) communicates immediately the focus of her "method" (chapter 4), and Elisabeth Howard's Vocal Power Academy (chapter 1) tells us something about her philosophy and what we might expect to achieve under her tutelage. Although the use of formal labels is least common among Australian teachers, Debbie Phyland's comment about the goals of training is particularly interesting. She says, "I don't think the method is as crucial as the outcome . . . if the sound is beautiful and moves us, then our method has been spot-on" (chapter 12).

The labeling of vocal qualities, along with discussions around resonance and registration, tend to be far less straightforward. Carry-over labels from centuries of classical training, like *chest* and *head*, are frequently used alongside newer labels from musical theatre, rock, and pop, like *belt, twang, mix, belt-mix, high belt*, and so forth. In addition, the continuing debate about the definition of these terms, both physiologically and aurally, adds to the confusion. Mary Hammond says, "All the terminology currently being used seems to be subjective. I think as long as the student and teacher agree on terminology, then that's okay" (chapter 7).

Certain of the terminology coined by Jo Estill (Estill Voice Training Systems) tends to be a part of the language of Australian singing teachers, even when they are not Estill trained. For example, the terms *twang, cry*, and *anchoring* are in common use. However, the Estill language is heard somewhat less frequently in the UK, and only occasionally in the United States.

MOVEMENT-RELATED WORK

Yoga has a strong, positive following among teachers in all three parts of the world; Feldenkrais is mentioned by interviewees in Australia and the UK.

The Alexander Technique is considered a positive and useful tool in the training of singers by well over half the teachers interviewed, whereas Pilates is given mixed reviews, especially by American teachers. Wendy LeBorgne says, "I think it's a good way to confuse a young singer . . . because it is a different type of breathing. [However] Pilates is great for core strengthening" (chapter 2). Mary Saunders-Barton comments enthusiastically, " . . . it's my favorite physical regimen" (chapter 5); yet Neil Semer says, "I think it can be a little rigid for singers" (chapter 6). From the UK, Mary Hammond says, "[Pilates] is very specific and you can target problems like, for example, a weak lower back, lower abdomen" (chapter 7), and Penni Harvey-Piper likes the image of *zip up* for "feeling that support" (chapter 8). Several Australian teachers also suggest that Pilates is a good thing to study; however, they do not relate the work directly to vocal technique.

Pilates training can be very different from one continent to another, and even from one practitioner to another, which helps to explain the contrasting views noted above. Of particular concern to voice specialists is the Pilates approach to breathing, which may or may not require noisy inhalations, accompanied by strongly contracted abdominal muscles, as in "belly button to the spine."

ADDITIONAL THOUGHTS

You will undoubtedly bring your own cultural view to the rich and multilayered nature of the interview material. My own perspective has been profoundly influenced by interaction with the sixteen master teachers who participated in this project. In addition, the opportunity to travel, teach, observe, see theatre, and talk with actors, singers, directors, dancers, movement specialists, and other theatre professionals has been an incredible learning adventure.

One of the most beautiful outcomes of this project has been the realization that we are all so similar and that we connect so easily. Venues may look different and the sound of the language may surprise us at times, but the passion is the same, the joy, and the supportive quality of the work. Elisabeth Howard (chapter 1) says, "I believe that anyone can learn how to sing, and sing beautifully at *any* age, and I have the need to prove this every day of my life." Gillyanne Kayes (chapter 9) says, "What drives me is enabling people's voices to work." And from Pat

Wilson (chapter 14), "What drives me is love . . . it's the one fuel that doesn't clog up the system . . . [and when] you burn that love, there's no toxic remains."

REFERENCES

Estill Voice Training Systems, www.evts.com.

Hammond, M. 2004. Conversations with colleagues. London.

Meylan, M. 2004. "Pop Music Is In: The Changing Sound of Musical Theatre." www.voicefoundation.org/library/popmusic.pdf.

18. Comparative Approaches to Training

When I was a student at the Central School of Speech and Drama, we had a singing class with Meribeth Bunch (Dayme). It was a strange class to me because, while I accepted physical, exploratory, and improvisatory work in actor training, my expectations of a singing class were deeply rooted in the classical studio. So one day, when Meribeth had us bouncing our voices off the wall and throwing them around the room, I rebelled and blurted out, "This is not a singing class at all!" Although Meribeth's exact response to my outburst is curiously blurred in memory, that day marked a turning point in my perspective on voice training and changed forever the way I would think about and teach singing.

Voice professionals and students alike frequently have little opportunity to venture outside their particular areas of performance expertise. Therefore, it seems appropriate at this point to back up a bit and consider briefly, three *worlds* of voice training that are often separated and even pitted against one another: classical singing, musical theatre, and voice for the actor. There are highly respected voice specialists today who say that musical theatre has nothing to do with classical training. Others, in this study and elsewhere, take an opposite view. Regardless of view, classical training—or the *idea* of classical training—is a significant point of reference for many teachers and performers in Western culture; thus its inclusion in this discussion.

CONTEXT

It is important to note from the outset that there are many different pedagogical approaches within each area of focus. Therefore, there are no single, or definitive, models, in terms of content. For example, vocal sound that is considered classical, as opposed to non-classical or contemporary commercial, includes a wide variety of vocal timbres produced by several distinctly different vocal techniques. However, there are practical and peripheral elements associated with each of the trainings that may help to distinguish one from the other.

For example, if I go to a classical singing lesson I don't have to think about what I'm going to wear. I can go in a skirt or even high heels, because I'll probably stand at the piano for most of the lesson. The teacher will likely sit at the piano to play the vocalises, and may or may not have an accompanist come in to play the arias or other material I am preparing. In addition to a piano, there will be a mirror in the room, often full length, for observing various physical aspects of the technical training. At the end of the lesson (usually an hour in length), there will be a brief discussion of the work I am to do before the next session, words of thanks, and I'll pay for the lesson with cash or a check. Fees for individual lessons vary from one part of the country to another and from one country to another, but $75–$100 an hour is about average.

If I book a lesson with a musical theatre specialist (keeping in mind that many of these teachers train a variety of styles), I can also expect to work one on one for about an hour. The teaching room will look similar to the classical studio, but may include some movement-related equipment and/or microphones. Chances are I'll have been to one or more dance classes during the day and if I'm wearing heels, I'll probably remove them as quickly as possible! Casual clothes that allow for easy movement are recommended. Although I will likely stand by the piano for part of the hour, I may start on the floor, for example, doing breathing exercises based on the Accent Method, or tremor work from Fitzmaurice Destructuring, or I may sit on a big ball as I begin to vocalize. In other words, the lesson will tend to be physically oriented as it relates directly to my career as a triple threat actor/singer/dancer. The teacher will probably sit at the piano to play the vocal exercises and, again, may or may not use an accompanist for the work on repertoire. The fee will be about the same as for the classical lesson.

Study with a theatre voice teacher can take more than one form. I may either work one on one, or I can join a class of, say, six to twenty participants for weekly sessions or for an intensive workshop of several days. Casual attire is again appropriate, usually sweats or dancewear, because the work is movement-related. If it is a lesson, the room may be small; if it is a class, the room may be a dance studio, a stage, or any other available space. There may or may not be a piano or mirror in the room, and singing will not necessarily be a part of the training. As with other skill-development work, exercises are likely to precede a focus on repertoire. The fee for a private lesson will be about the same as for musical theatre or classical training. Tuition for intensive workshops averages $100 a day, and individual classes vary widely in cost from teacher to teacher.

PEDAGOGICAL OBJECTIVES

One of the goals of classical singing is a *beautiful* sound, with each note well crafted, which works magnificently for a wide range of material. However, in a stress-based language like English, equal attention to every syllable tends to flatten out the natural inflections of speech to such a degree that we frequently require subtitles or program notes in order to follow along. The same phenomenon occurs in musical theatre when singers focus more on the sound they are producing than on what they are saying. Actors, as well, often sing very differently from the way they speak, especially if they are not comfortable singing. Nevertheless, sound is of paramount importance to the classical singer and audiences go to classical performances in order to *listen*.

Another goal of classical training is the development of a vocal *line*, or the ability to sing without "breaks" or obvious changes of quality, throughout the entire pitch range. Having a line to the voice is also extremely valuable to the musical theatre singer and to the actor. Mark Meylan (2005) says that singers in musical theatre need to be able to sing any note in their range to any vowel to any vocal quality to any vocal dynamic, which implies having multiple vocal lines! For the actor, being able to move easily and smoothly throughout a wide pitch range opens up additional character choices and is particularly useful in dialect work. However, both in musical theatre and in nonmusical productions, homogeneity in vocal quality is not always desirable.

The ability to "project" the sound is also critical to classical singing, which is traditionally not amplified (although some performances are miked nowadays). Musical theatre singers also train and audition acoustically, although their sound may not fill the space in the same way that classical singing does. Musical theatre productions are usually miked—even when miking is not necessary for the space. However, one does occasionally hear an unmiked performance, for example, in training programs, and the sound in such performances can be incredibly wonderful! Jean Callaghan (2004) notes that many people today have never heard a live voice and have no idea what the voice can do. Actors in theatre, like classical singers, must be able to be heard without microphones at any level of volume, in any style, accent, or dialect, and in any venue.

In all three trainings, tutors work to help students release unnecessary tension, strengthen appropriate habits of alignment and breath management, access a wide vocal range, and develop the muscularity necessary for efficient articulation. Individual technical elements are then synthesized and focused into communication that regularly includes the medium of text.

REPERTOIRE

Voice in actor training includes the analysis and performance of dramatic, poetic, and prose texts from a variety of style periods. Classical training for singers includes a similar range of work, dramatic texts coming primarily from opera, poetic texts from Lieder and other art songs, and prose texts from recitative. Also included in the classical repertoire of some singers is contemporary, or *new* music, which often veers away from the beautiful and connects the performer instinctively with the actor's perspective and theatre voice. From the advent of Sprechstimme early in the twentieth century, along with the development of serial techniques and the use of atonality, *beauty* as an invariable characteristic of classical sound was effectively challenged. A hundred years later, now on the musical theatre scene, the singer's classically oriented *legit* sound is being similarly challenged. In both cases, the demand for different and exceptional use of the voice moves singers directly into the world of theatre voice, where virtually any sound that is safely produced may be useful.

MUSICIANSHIP

Classical singers nowadays need to be quite good at reading what is on the page, interpreting stylistic differences, and dealing with rhythmic complexities. Time was when they simply got by on the beauty of their voices and even the most celebrated opera singers learned their music by rote. I recall vividly the surprise, if not shock, of conductors when they realized I could work the same as instrumentalists. Singers still have the reputation for being the weakest members of the sight-singing class, and many musical theatre singers regularly learn their music by rote. However, one must remember that while classical singers are focusing primarily on singing, musical theatre performers are also learning to dance and act and—most recently—to play other musical instruments!

Music theory classes make up a significant part of the core curriculum of conservatory training programs for classical singers, and musical theatre students take basic courses in musicianship. Actors, on the other hand, frequently have little or no formal training in music, so when they are required to sing in the course of a production, they simply wing it. More and more training programs, though, are beginning to include singing in the actor's curriculum, and when basic musicianship classes are offered along with the practical work, an important dimension is added to the actor's overall package.

For all the enormous benefit provided by formal training, however, there is no substitute for raw talent and the instincts of a performer. The ability to hear and reproduce sounds accurately is essential for singers in any arena, and being able to feel and understand rhythms at a level deeper than the intellect is invaluable. At the same time, balancing instinct with a degree of technical knowledge tends to strengthen performers in all three areas of voice training.

SUMMARY

Classical singing, musical theatre, and voice for the actor are both intimately connected and deeply separated. Common elements form the basis of technical training across curricula, yet the goals and ideals of training depend upon the medium for which the work is designed. Consistently beautiful sound remains a major focus of most classical work, while musical theatre singers are, of necessity, embracing an extraordinary range of vocal qualities. The physical environment for teaching and learning is considerably more movement-oriented in actor training than in classical singing, and musical theatre falls somewhere in between. Voice training for the actor may or may not include singing, whereas classical work and musical theatre focus primarily on singing. It is in the area of extended voice use that the three trainings meet most efficiently and overlap both technically and aesthetically. Current musical theatre styles, along with contemporary classical works, require singers to duplicate virtually every vocal utterance in the actor's repertoire, including speech and chant, calls, shouts, and screams. Thus, the line between speaking and singing is effectively blurred, at least momentarily.

REFERENCES

Callaghan, J. 2004. Conversations with colleagues. Sydney.

Meylan, M. 2005. Master classes. Australian National Association of Teachers of Singing. Sydney.

19. PRACTICAL APPLICATIONS

This project grew out of my passion for connecting the dots between speaking and singing and, more especially, between actor training and the training of singers. Singing techniques, as a normal, unobtrusive part of theatre voice work, can make a huge difference in an actor's available pitch range, confidence level, articulatory skill, and total integration of body and voice. Singers, on the other hand, need the textual skills and range of vocal qualities regularly included in theatre voice training, and the movement aspect of that work can transform their presence on stage.

Acting students frequently say to me, "Will you do a singing warm-up for us, Joan? That's when we really feel warmed up." And Graham Welch (2005) describes a study in which participants went from an extended voice class in an acting program, directly into an opera rehearsal and found their voices far more open and resonant than usual. Their level of energy had also increased. These instances are relatively rare, however, and in most teaching situations it's still this or that, one or the other. While the same technical elements figure prominently both in singing pedagogy and voice for the actor, differences in perspective from music to theatre frequently serve to obscure the common ground and interconnectedness of the two disciplines.

Theatre voice tends to be highly process-oriented and is designed to provide essential support for the rest of the actor's work. It is about securing the technical means to go virtually any direction in the course of an acting class or production. On the other hand, singing pedagogy encompasses more of the performance itself and is, of necessity, more prescriptive in terms of what the voice is programmed to do in each given circumstance.

This chapter focuses on the practical transfer of techniques from one training to another, and acknowledges basic pedagogical concepts that are valid, regardless of the performance medium. The stories, exercises, and discussions that follow are based in part on my own response to the wealth of material in the interview chapters. They are intended to act as a springboard for *your* imagination, so please feel free to use them as you discover other integrative possibilities.

SEEING THE CONNECTIONS

Jeremy was a first-year graduate actor who'd come into the MFA program from another field. He was usually "in his head" and when he spoke onstage it was difficult to understand him. Still he shrugged off most of the articulation work and did not improve. Then he was cast as Judd Fry in *Oklahoma!* and things began to change. He couldn't believe the way the musical theatre students spoke and sang. "Their consonants are just right out there!" And he was smart enough to bring his own work up to their level. I seldom gave him another note about articulation.

Students in a second-semester course were working on a project that required both extended voice use and accurate dialect work. When an actor was having particular difficulty, I said to her, "You need more space in the throat. The sound is a bit tight." She did the scene again and it was great. I said, "What did you do?" She said, "I just thought about what I do when I sing."

Jean Callaghan (2004) refers to singing as an extended use of the voice, and Dr. Robert Sataloff (2003) has called singing an aerobic vocal activity. It is in the area of extended voice use that singing and voice for the actor meet most directly, especially in terms of resonance. There are similarities, for example, between the shape of the vocal tract for *laughing* and *crying*, and a variety of vocal qualities, both spoken and sung. *Shouting*, on the other hand, is equivalent to *calling* without extending the vowels (and, by the way, is most effective in a low to medium range rather than high in the voice). Tutored shouting also has huge amounts in common with the forward "placement," efficient breath work, and sense of an open pipe, or ease in the throat, required for various kinds of belting. And the heart of a good *scream* is a fabulous high note!

Techniques from theatre voice tend to overlap the work in musical theatre, which is handy for the performer. Accents and dialects, for example, serve easily as a reference for differentiating voice qualities, and knowledge of the IPA (International Phonetic Alphabet) provides a shortcut to the communication of specific pronunciations. Musical theatre, on the other hand, forces the actor to commit fully to a text so that the communication of a lyric is absolutely clear, regardless of the physicality of the piece and the volume level of the orchestra!

CROSSOVER TECHNIQUES

Each of the major technical areas of voice training offers opportunities for sharing information, perspectives, techniques, and specific exercises. In the next section, comments from interviewees serve as points of departure for discussions of crossover possibilities and integrative work.

ALIGNMENT AND BREATHING

Joan Lader (chapter 3) says breathing and alignment are inseparable, and Debbie Phyland (chapter 12) says, "The breathing will often look after itself as long as the inspirations aren't audible." I recall vividly a workshop led by Anita Downey (London 1990), in which the opening exercise had us jogging about the room and using our voices in a variety of ways. When we stopped, Anita said (paraphrased), "The body knows how to breathe in. Our job is to use the breath out." And indeed it is! Most vocal work is done on the breath out. Noisy inhalations obstruct the airway and actually make it more difficult for us to breathe quickly and easily in performance. There are exceptions, of course—for example, in some highly emotional scenes—but inhalation on a regular basis is a quiet matter.

The following exercise from theatre voice is great for developing an awareness of technical efficiency and may be useful in any area of voice training:

∾

Sit very quiet and centered on a box or stool with your feet on the floor. If you are working on your own, sit in front of a mirror. Think yourself tall, wide, and flexible—elegant, if you will. If you are working in a class, have three or four other students monitor your physical activity. Key areas to observe (hands-on if you like) are the head and neck, shoulders, rib cage, abdomen, and feet. Speak or sing a monologue or simply converse (as if on stage) with another member of the class. Then change the vocal activity, being sure to sing as well as speak. Note any differences in physical use as you move from speaking to singing, or from casual conversation to a prepared monologue. Then mix it up. Sing your conversation or monologue and speak the lyrics to your song as if they'd never been set to music (so *not* in the rhythm of the song!). Enjoy the sensation of being both energized and still. Your breathing should be quiet and unobtrusive, as you release all extraneous effort and do only what is required to communicate.

∞

Along with efficient alignment and inspiration, Penni Harvey-Piper (chapter 8) advocates a *low* breath and refers to the Pilates image of *zip up* for "feeling that support" from the abdominal muscles. The same image does not work for every performer, of course, but the idea is to activate the deepest layer of abdominal muscle, the transversus, along with more exterior muscles, for core stability (see Wendy LeBorgne, chapter 2) as well as breath management. Ultrasound imaging (Blake & Grey 2007) now allows us to view the activity of the abdominal layers, and the sound itself tells us immediately whether or not the voice is "supported."

The Accent Method is particularly applicable to the idea of support. Better known in the UK (chapter 9) and Australia (chapter 12) than in the United States, the technique was developed for voice therapy and includes "isolation of the muscle activity of breathing" (Harris 2007, conference handout). Repeated rhythmic patterns, or *accents*, graded from simple to complex, are used first with an unvoiced fricative (e.g., /s/), then with other vocal sounds, to develop strength and efficiency in the abdominal muscles. This aspect of the method relates directly to breath management and deserves far more space than this chapter permits.

In actor training, we speak of connecting the body and voice, and appropriate abdominal activity is often key to that connection, especially in the low- to mid-pitch range. The same is true for singing. However, *what* is appropriate *when* is influenced by a variety of factors, including the vocal medium and the performance venue.

The exercises below are distinctly crossover in nature. They help to develop an awareness of abdominal activity and teach the performer to release the abs quickly in order to *allow* the breath in.

∞

On all fours (back flat, head/neck comfortably free, elbows not locked), speak gentle staccato sounds on "huh" or "hah" (one short, *clear* note per exhalation—so the /h/ is silent). Don't overwork. If the belly is free, the abs will engage easily, and be sure to *let go* of the abs between sounds! Then, using the unvoiced fricative /sh/, do a simple rhythmic pattern (of accents) instead of a single sound on each exhalation, for example, short, short, short, long, as in a three-beat pickup to a 6/8 bar. Then, if you like, play with bits of text, spoken or sung, making sure that you begin each phrase with the same gentle abdominal action as with the staccatos.

Stand monkey fashion with feet apart, knees bent, hands on thighs, leaning slightly forward with a flat back. Start with repeated staccatos and/or accent patterns, using an unvoiced or voiced fricative (e.g., /s/ or /z/); then speak or sing with the same abdominal initiation of the vocal activity and quick release of the abs between phrases.

Sit cross-legged on the floor doing staccatos on a variety of vowel sounds and playing throughout your range. Feel free to use your arms and upper body as well. Then sing a song (still seated), using the same essential abdominal actions as in your playful warm-up. In the song, of course, you will do one entire phrase per exhalation and will likely encounter a variety of accent patterns. Remember to stay released and at ease as you communicate from center, from your core.

∞

RANGE AND RESONANCE

Actors seldom think about their pitch range when they're speaking, but will tell you right away that they have no high notes or that their voice won't go low or that they sound weak in the middle when they sing. Singers, on the other hand, tend to use a wide pitch range when they sing but limit themselves to a few notes when they speak. Additionally, they may be unaware of the amazing range of vocal qualities available to them when they are not singing! Actors develop and use a pitch range of at least two and a half to three octaves for material that is not sung. Classical work, in particular, makes huge demands in terms of pitch, quality, and tempo, and experimental pieces frequently require extended voice use. Yet when it comes to specific pitches, range is often a big item for actors, both psychologically and physically.

Helping performers to deal with that item and overcome the blocks that tend to form around it are primary concerns for voice specialists in every area of training. Mary Saunders-Barton (chapter 5) says, "Clearly a great deal of my time in the studio is spent trying to help students create a thoroughly blended voice." Amanda Colliver (chapter 15) uses a particularly interesting approach to intervals. She says, "Disconnection is the primary symptom of *buying into* distance, so I help students to sing the intervals as though they were much smaller; for example, an octave jump as a third or even as a semitone. This, in turn, keeps the voice connected and the resonance intact."

Keeping the voice connected is one way of describing a vocal *line*, or integrated pitch range in which there are no obvious "breaks" from top to bottom, or bottom to top. Jeannette LoVetri (chapter 4) focuses on "balancing the registers" of the voice to help singers move smoothly and safely throughout a wide range. William Vennard (1967) used an image that I shall never forget. He said you can fill a test tube with half earth and half water, but what you want, ideally, is to shake the tube vigorously so that you have a clay mixture throughout. A bit more earth at the bottom and a bit more water at the top, but earth and water throughout.

For singers and actors alike, *blending* the voice is usually easier in the context of movement. Pat Wilson (chapter 14) says, "I think phonation comes most safely and easily out of a moved body." I would suggest further that high notes tend to be easier in rounded or curled positions, and low notes release "naturally" as you open or arch the body. Glissandi are invaluable for moving throughout the range, especially on hums of various descriptions, tongue and/or lip trills, and on vowels, with or without reference to singing.

Mary Saunders-Barton (chapter 5) says that what is expected now at musical theatre auditions is quite different from what was required even a few years ago. Women, for example, are no longer asked to separate "soprano" and "belt," but are expected to put it all together as in a vocal line, or *mix*. Classical singers have always developed a line; the *seamless voice* is one of the hallmarks of classical technique. However, singers in musical theatre have tended to separate the voice into parts, sometimes deliberately, but often because they have been unaware of the possibility of integrating the entire range.

In actor training, we regularly refer to a *neutral*, or a place of physical balance, where the performer feels centered, alive, and ready to move in any direction. Similarly, the term vocal *line* indicates a neutral, or connected, position vocally, and, for actors, finding that line is often key to the realization that they can *sing* as well as speak over a very wide pitch range. Michael Lugering (2006) suggests that having a secure neutral frees the actor to play off-balance physicality with greater skill and imagination. Likewise, a blended, or connected, voice frees the actor/singer to make choices vocally.

Singers in musical theatre regularly choose to mix the voice in ways that are distinctly different from the blended sounds of a classical singer. Wendy LeBorgne (chapter 2) suggests that in musical theatre the thyrovocalis muscle (the deepest layer of the vocal folds, analogous to earth in the test tube) is slightly more active throughout most of the range. This helps to explain physiologically the wonderful, gutsy sounds we associate with many non-classical styles.

For singers and speakers who perform all their lives without formal training, blending or mixing the voice is often unconscious and truly "natural." We have much to learn from these performers! For the majority of students in drama and music schools, however, there is a conscious journey to be taken. Teachers act as invaluable guides along that journey, and the same method is not right for every performer.

The following exercises introduce the actor to a vocal line in a very non-threatening way. They are useful for singers as well because they involve the whole body, reinforce the work on alignment, and develop an ability to use the entire pitch range without actually singing! In addition, they require a certain abandon that is uniquely valuable for performers.

∞

19–1

Begin on your knees. Put your hands on the floor palms down, then place the top of your head on the floor with no weight on the head. Meow like a little cat very gently. It helps to wrinkle your nose and play! Once you have an easy, high sound, continue to meow as you move either to sitting on your heels or standing on your knees (Figure 19-1). Then, with both hands/arms moving slowly from high above your head (palms forward) to low about your pelvis, meow (glissando) through your range—top to bottom—staying with the first two vowels of the meow triphthong until the very end. Your mouth will be spread laterally, cheeks up, eyes alive! This is just the edge of a sound, the center, or the connecting link that helps to integrate the voice from top to bottom. It's rather like a silk thread, so resist the temptation to get heavy at any point. Repeat the extended meow several times.

Sit cross-legged on the floor with your back upright, rather than rounded. (If you have difficulty with the cross-legged position, try sitting on a yoga block or zafu so that your spine can lengthen easily.) Then extend one leg diagonally and move the entire torso from the pelvis, toward that leg. Lower the torso gently over the leg just to see where you are at the moment, *keeping a flat back—even if you move very little.* If you need to bend the knee a bit, that's fine, but do not round the back to touch the toes! (1) Then, using the arm opposite from the extended leg, swoop or dive downward toward the leg and allow the follow-through to complete the circle upward before you swoop down again (Figure 19-2). (The main action is in your hip socket, so you are leading from the pelvis.) Using an unvoiced fricative (e.g., /s/ or /f/), make a nice noisy exhalation on the

19–2

swoop. Repeat three times (so four times in all). *Be sure to keep both buttocks on the floor.* (2) Continue the swooping action, but this time place the hand on the floor and bring the opposite arm over your head without lifting the shoulder (Figure 19-3). Don't flop the arm, but rather, move as if you're working against resistance. At the same time, allow your voice to swoop high to low on a very bright /a/ glissando and don't be shy! Repeat three times. (3) Glissando again high to low on an /a/ as you repeat the physical action to the hand on the floor; then go up on the knee of the bent leg as you

19–3

reach the opposite arm over your

photography by Michael Puoci   *19–4*

head (Figure 19-4). Release the belly to allow the breath to "drop in." Then glissando low to high as you swoop downward with the reaching arm and move the entire torso over or toward the extended leg. Repeat on the opposite side. Then go into a crouch, or child's pose with arms stretched out in front of you. Continue to play through the voice on glissando hums, and feel free to stretch and move in the process.

Note there is an underlying rhythm, part (1) being in a count of two, and parts (2) and (3) being in a count of four. This exercise encourages full excursion of the rib cage one side at a time, stretches and activates all of the abdominal muscles, helps to release tightness in the groin muscles (which directly affect the head/neck alignment), and effectively centers the action of the body and breath in the pelvis. In addition, it uses the principle of rounding for high notes and opening for low, as it extends the pitch range in both directions.

∞

TEXT AND ARTICULATION

Actors and singers alike frequently consider the text of a work their primary source for inspiration, understanding, clarity, and direction. Jean Callaghan (2004) takes that a step further and speaks of "the music and the language and the body as a text." Amanda Colliver (chapter 15) says, "It's easy to get caught up in making beautiful sounds rather than in what is being said. Neither one should compromise the other, and when the components of both music and text come together, we have something greater than either one on its own." And Liz Pascoe (chapter 16) says, ". . . we look at the relationship of the musical text with the word text. Which is more important in this particular song? Or are they of equal importance? What *sound quality* does the text demand?"

Sound quality is a very big topic in musical theatre and is addressed more thoroughly in the interview chapters. However, it is worth noting here that sound quality for the actor has to do with the body and life of the character and can be a very conscious choice. In musical theatre, on the other hand, the singer may be expected to produce a specific sound quality, and the expectations may change depending upon the circumstances and location of the production, for example, the United States, Britain, or Australia (see Cultural Perspectives, chapter 17).

Gillyanne Kayes provides a detailed analysis of consonant/vowel relationships in her book, *Singing and the Actor*, and even assigns specific time values to individual consonants in a song. For example, a voiced consonant might occupy a quarter or half the note value of a syllable. Her approach to language is equally valuable for spoken text, especially when actors are working within the rich fabric of classical material. Also, the assignment of note values to specific vowel sounds can be a godsend for American actors who struggle with the idea of differences in vowel length.

Regardless of the performance medium, "It's the weight on a syllable that matters," according to Penni Harvey-Piper (chapter 8), and I would take that a step further, to the use of operative words. Penni says a lyric must sound natural. "It must be the way that people would [say] that phrase if they were just acting it." So both in speaking and singing, there are soft, throwaway syllables—for example, little connecting words like *a, the, in, and*, and *as*. And in a stress-based language like English, there are usually one or two words per phrase that are emphasized, or *operative*, because of the context.

THE ACTING DIMENSION

Mary Saunders-Barton (chapter 5) says, "In musical theatre you have to act, sing, and dance, in that order of priority . . . the singing and dancing skills are at the service of the dramatic imperative . . . Act, tell the story, or nobody's interested."

Acting can be approached from a variety of perspectives, and this is not a book about acting. Still, there are principles from actor training that are highly valuable for singers to know. For example, when classical singers consider the acting dimension, the word *emotion* or *emotional* tends to come up immediately, and in some cases, the word *gesture* is also operative. Actors and musical theatre singers, on the other hand, tend to come from a different direction and speak of *objective* or *intention, tactics*, and/or of playing *actions*, in which case the focus is on *doing*, rather than *being*.

Musical theatre specialists are often aware of both perspectives and use whatever is appropriate to move themselves and/or their students toward a desired result. However, if the actor's approach is not among the singer's tools, his or her habitual result can be beautiful sound turned inward, rather than something exciting and captivating that is *happening* in a theatre space. Craig Carnelia says, "Emotion is something we inadvertently feel when we do what we do, and if we plan that ahead of time we get something that is canned" (2006). In other words, emotion is a response to action. It is where we wind up—in our bodies—not where we start in our heads. So if we predetermine that emotion, it is no longer a response and comes across as fake.

Likewise, *gesture*, in the sense of appropriate movements of the hands and arms, is not regularly a part of theatre voice terminology, although it does figure into some acting styles, for example, commedia dell' arte and Restoration comedy. Physicality for the actor involves the entire body and is determined largely by the role; therefore, the actor's movements, aside from blocking, tend to be spontaneous and integral to the action, rather than preplanned. Singers, on the other hand, frequently consider voice, body, facial expressions and hand/arm gestures in a more conscious manner.

Following is an improvisatory exercise that can be used with virtually any material, for example monologues, songs, or scenes, to demonstrate the difference between playing an emotional state and playing an action. It requires a partner or partners. Gesture will take care of itself if you simply allow the body to do what it will in the context of the exercise.

∞

Using a short section of the piece, do it being angry or sad or happy or upset, and see how it feels. Ask your partner for feedback. Then do it to kick or seduce or intrigue or surprise your partner and observe the difference. Again, ask your partner and/or other members of the class for feedback.

∞

Audiences usually find the second approach the more interesting of the two.

Expanding the View

Trainings that interact and support, rather than conflict, empower us all to work at a higher level of creativity. Being able to use the whole voice, for example, can be enormously freeing—not to mention professionally advantageous—regardless of the performance emphasis. The crossover benefits for voice specialists are virtually limitless, and the advantages for performers go far beyond lessons and classes.

Techniques that transfer most easily from singing pedagogy to actor training characteristically demonstrate an awareness of the total range of the actor's attention and integrate naturally into the physicality of the actor's perspective. Neil Semer's (chapter 6) approach is particularly comprehensive in that it starts with the body and includes group warm-ups on the floor, focusing on breathing and on centering the entire being for the act of communicating. Attention to repertoire then balances the performer's understanding of technique with style and performance acuity.

For the actor, voice is not the main event, although it is usually a significant contributor to the event and in a few cases—for example, in Dylan Thomas's *Under Milk Wood*—it is the star! In classical singing, however, voice is nearly always the main event and in musical theatre it frequently functions as the event of the moment. Awareness of these distinctly different perspectives is critical for the specialist working in more than one area of voice training.

Fortunately, we are in a field that is never static, and it is highly unlikely that we will ever understand every aspect of voice in performance. Therefore, we will continue to teach and perform from a variety of angles and will be responsive to the respective markets with which we interface. Nevertheless, our ability to acknowledge one another and the connective links within our respective pedagogies somehow changes the equation, and sets up a new paradigm that could positively affect the training environment of a new generation of performers.

REFERENCES

Blake, E., & Grey, J. 2007. "Ultrasound Imaging of Abdominal Support Mechanisms Whilst Voicing: Proposed Effects on Subglottic Pressure and Laryngeal Mobility." In *Performance Breath: An Essential Exploration of Body, Voice & Word*. London: RADA Enterprises.

Callaghan, J. 2005, 2004. Conversations with colleagues, Sydney.

Carnelia, C. 2006. "Music Theater Performance Techniques." National Association of Teachers of Singing Conference, Minneapolis.

Downey, A. 1990. Workshop for ADVS candidates. Central School of Speech & Drama, London.

Harris, D., & Harris, S. 2007. "Introduction to the Accent Method." In *Performance Breath: An Essential Exploration of Body, Voice & Word*. London: RADA Enterprises.

Kayes, G. 2004. *Singing and the Actor*, 2nd ed. London: A & C Black (UK); Routledge (USA and Canada).

Lugering, M. 2006. "The Expressive Actor." Dance Theatre Workshop. New York.

Melton, J., & Tom, K. 2003. *ONE VOICE: Integrating Singing Technique and Theatre Voice Training*. Portsmouth: Heinemann.

Sataloff, R. 2003. "Medical Evaluation and Treatment of Professional Singers: An Overview." Voice Foundation Symposium. Philadelphia.

Vennard, W. 1967. *Singing: The Mechanism and the Technic*. Boston: Carl Fischer.

Welch, G. 2005. "Delivering Young Voice." Joint Workshop, Australian National Association of Teachers of Singing/Australian Voice Association, Sydney.

APPENDIX
Voice Associations and Foundations

Australian National Association of Teachers of Singing (ANATS), P.O. Box 576, Crows Nest NSW 1585, Australia, www.anats.org.au.

Australian Voice Association (AVA), General Secretariat, 2nd floor, 11-19 Bank Place, Melbourne, VIC 3000, Australia; ava@vicnet.au, www.australiavoiceassociation.com.au.

British Voice Association (BVA), Institute of Laryngology and Otology, 330 Gray's Inn Road, London WC1XSEE, UK, www.british-voice-association.com.

Canadian Voice Care Foundation (CVCF), 2828 Toronto Crescent NW, Calgary, AB T2N 3W2, Canada, cvcf@shaw.ca.

National Association of Teachers of Singing (NATS), 4745 Sutton Park Court, Suite 201, Jacksonville, FL 32224, USA, www.nats.org.

New Zealand Association of Teachers of Singing (NEWZATS), Box 29045, Ngaio, Wellington, NZ, www.newzats.org.nz.

Voice and Speech Trainers Association (VASTA), United States. www.vasta.org.

Voice Foundation, 1721 Pine Street, Philadelphia, PA 19103, www.voicefoundation.org.

ABOUT THE AUTHOR

JOAN MELTON is a pioneer in the integration of singing techniques and voice training for the actor. She is one of the few voice professionals in the world with a firm grasp of both theatre voice and singing training. A Master Teacher of the Fitzmaurice approach to theatre voice training, she lectures internationally and has taught at leading drama and music centers in the United States, Great Britain, Ireland, Australia, and New Zealand. She initiated and developed

© Mitchell Rose Photography

the Voice/Movement program (1996–2006) for the Department of Theatre and Dance at California State University, Fullerton, and is a published author and composer with performance credits in theatre, opera, television, and voiceover. Trained at the Central School of Speech and Drama, London, Melton holds a PhD from the University of North Carolina, Chapel Hill. The author, with Kenneth Tom, PhD, of the groundbreaking book, *One Voice: Integrating Singing Technique and Theatre Voice Training* (Heinemann), Melton is currently based in NYC.

INDEX

Books from Allworth Press

Allworth Press is an imprint of Allworth Communications, Inc. Selected titles are listed below.

Acting Teachers of America: A Vital Tradition
by Ronald Rand and Luigi Scorcia (paperback, 6 × 9, 288 pages, $19.95)

Acting: Advanced Techniques for the Actor, Director, and Teacher.
by Terry Schreiber (paperback, 6 × 9, 256 pages, $19.95)

Movement for Actors
edited by Nicole Potter (paperback, 6 × 9, 288 pages, $19.95)

Making It on Broadway: Actor's Tales of Climbing to the Top
by David Wiener and Jodie Langel (paperback, 6 × 9, 288 pages, $19.95)

The Actor's Way: A Journey of Self-Discovery in Letters
by Benjamin Lloyd (paperback, 5 ½ × 8 ½, 224 pages, $16.95)

Clues to Acting Shakespeare, Second Edition
by Wesley Van Tassel (paperback, 6 × 9, 256 pages, $18.95)

Mastering Shakespeare: An Acting Class in Seven Scenes
by Scott Kaiser (paperback, 6 × 9, 256 pages, $19.95)

The Actor Rehearses: What to Do When and Why
by David Hlavsa (paperback, 6 × 9, 224 pages, $18.95)

Improv for Actors
by Dan Diggles (paperback, 6 × 9, 224 pages, $19.95)

Acting That Matters
by Barry Pineo (paperback, 6 × 9, 256 pages, $19.95)

To request a free catalog or order books by credit card, call 1-800-491-2808. To see our complete catalog on the World Wide Web, or to order online for a 20 percent discount, you can find us at **www.allworth.com.**